Editor

Eric Migliaccio

Illustrator

Vicki Frazier

Cover Artist

Brenda DiAntonis

Editor in Chief

Ina Massler Levin, M.A.

Creative Director

Karen J. Goldfluss, M.S. Ed.

Art Production Manager

Kevin Barnes

Art Coordinator

Renée Christine Yates

Imaging

Rosa C. See

Publisher

Mary D. Smith, M.S. Ed.

Author

Debra J. Housel, M.S. Ed.

Teacher Created Resources, Inc.

6421 Industry Way
Westminster, CA 92683
www.teachercreated.com

ISBN: 978-1-4206-8093-5

© 2008 Teacher Created Resources, Inc.
Made in U.S.A.

Table of Contents

Introduction

Content Area Lessons Using Graphic Organizers is designed to save you time and effort. It contains complete lessons that meet the standards for your grade level in reading, writing, science, geography, history, and math. Each lesson uses a different graphic organizer. Thus, if you do all the lessons in this book and never use another graphic organizer, your students will have worked with 23 different graphic organizers. This provides significant exposure to these important educational tools.

Graphic organizers show the organization of concepts and the relationships among them. They offer a clear depiction of data, which research has proven is more memorable than pages of notes. They show students "how it all fits together," which is much more effective than having them try to memorize bits of data without thoroughly understanding the context. Showing how information is organized helps students—especially English-language learners and those with reading disabilities—focus on content instead of semantics and grammar.

Compelling Reasons to Use Graphic Organizers

Research shows that graphic organizers actually improve students' creative, analytical, and critical-thinking skills. Why? Graphic organizers help students of all ages to process information. Processing information is a complex skill requiring the ability to identify essential ideas; decide which details are relevant and which are irrelevant; understand how information is structured; and perhaps most importantly of all, figure out how data relates to other information or situations. Processing information demands the use of such higher-level thinking skills as making decisions, drawing conclusions, and forming inferences.

Substantial amounts of research support the fact that graphic organizers increase the understanding and retention of critical information for students who range from gifted to those with learning disabilities. This means that using graphic organizers may meet the needs of the many different learners in your classroom without the time-consuming task of individualization.

The visual element inherent in graphic organizers supports three cognitive-learning theories: dual coding theory, schema theory, and cognitive load theory.

- **Dual coding theory** acknowledges that presenting information in both visual and verbal form improves recall and recognition. Graphic organizers do both effectively.

- **Schema theory** states that a learner's prediction based on his or her background knowledge (schema) is crucial for acquiring new information. This is why readers have a hard time comprehending material in an unfamiliar subject even when they know the meaning of the separate words in the text. Graphic organizers' ability to show relationships builds upon and increases students' schema.

- **Cognitive load theory** stresses that a student's short-term memory has limitations in the amount of data it can simultaneously hold. Since any instructional information must first be processed by short-term memory, for long-term memory (schema acquisition) to occur, instruction must reduce the short-term memory load. Thus, teaching methods that cut down on the demands of short-term memory give the brain a better opportunity to facilitate activation of long-term memory. Graphic organizers fit the bill perfectly.

Graphic organizers are appearing more often in standardized tests and state assessments. Giving your students practice with the variety of graphic organizers offered in this book can help them to achieve better scores on these assessments.

Introduction *(cont.)*

How to Use This Book

Each lesson in *Content Area Lessons Using Graphic Organizers* is designed to be used where it fits into your curriculum. Whenever you start a new unit, check to see if one of these lessons will work with your topic. Where applicable, reading levels based on the Flesch-Kincaid formula are included.

The lessons often require that you make a transparency and student copies of the graphic organizers located on the CD. Any other necessary materials will be stated in the lesson. These might include such things as highlighters, index cards, poster board, scissors, glue, and zipper bags. If possible, when writing on the overhead transparency, use different colors to differentiate between specific sections. This is another way to help your students to visualize data.

The graphic organizers give as much space as possible for the students to write. However, if some of your students have large handwriting, make an overhead transparency of the blank graphic organizer and display it on the overhead. Then have a school aide or the students tape a sheet of construction paper where the overhead projects and copy the format onto the paper. This will give them more room to write.

If you are just starting to use graphic organizers, you may worry that they are time-consuming. Keep in mind that it is time well spent. Graphic organizers provide meaningful instruction that gives your students an advantage in comprehending and remembering data. By using graphic organizers you are teaching not just content but thought processes. Your students are learning how to learn—an invaluable skill that will serve them well for the rest of their lives.

Be Flexible and Creative

The graphic organizers included in *Content Area Lessons Using Graphic Organizers* have many uses; they are not limited to the lessons or subject area in which they appear. Most of these graphic organizers can be used or modified to fit the needs of other lessons or subjects. Sometimes a student will self-advocate by asking you to make copies of a certain kind for use in other areas. You may find that a challenged student enjoys and learns best using one particular type. Be flexible and creative in your use of graphic organizers.

If you have a class that really enjoys graphic organizers, you could opt to evaluate student learning by letting the students create their own graphic organizers. You may be pleasantly surprised by your students' abilities to make meaningful graphics that show interrelationships in a more effective way than they could explain in writing.

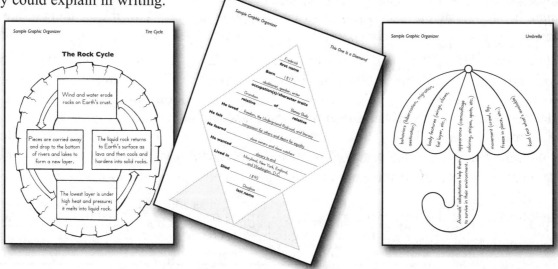

Standards Correlation Chart

Each lesson in this book meets at least one of the following standards and benchmarks:

Standards and Benchmarks	Pages
Math	
Standard 2. Understands and applies basic and advanced properties of the concepts of numbers	
• **Benchmark 1.** Understands basic number theory concepts (e.g., prime and composite numbers, factors, mutliples, odd and even numbers, divisibility)	8–10
• **Benchmark 3.** Understands the basic difference between odd and even numbers	8–10
Standard 3. Uses basic and advanced procedures while performing the processes of computation	
• **Benchmark 1.** Adds, subtracts, multiplies, and divides whole numbers and decimals	8–13
• **Benchmark 5.** Determines the effects of addition, subtraction, multiplication, and division on size and order of numbers	14–16
• **Benchmark 6.** Understands the properties of and the relationships among addition, subtraction, multiplication, and division	14–16
• **Benchmark 7.** Solves real-world problems involving number operations (e.g., computations with dollars and cents)	8–13
Science	
Standard 2. Understands Earth's composition and structure	
• **Benchmark 1.** Knows how features on Earth's surface are constantly changed by a combination of slow and rapid processes (e.g., weathering, erosion, transport, and deposition of sediment caused by waves, wind, water, and ice; landslides, volcanic eruptions, earthquakes, drought)	17–20
• **Benchmark 2.** Knows that smaller rocks come from the breakage and weathering of larger rocks and bedrock	17–20
• **Benchmark 5.** Knows that fossils provide evidence about the plants and animals that lived long ago and the nature of the environment at that time	21–24
Standard 3. Understands the composition of the universe and Earth's place in it	
• **Benchmark 1.** Knows that night and day are caused by Earth's rotation on its axis	49–52
Standard 5. Understands the structure and function of cells and organisms	
• **Benchmark 3.** Knows that the behavior of individual organisms is influenced by internal cues (e.g., hunger) and external cues (e.g., changes in the environment), and that humans and other organisms have senses that help them to detect these cues	25–28
Standard 6. Understands relationships among organisms and their physical environment	
• **Benchmark 1.** Knows the organization of simple food chains and food webs	61–64
• **Benchmark 2.** Knows that changes in the environment can have different effects on different organisms	25–28, 61–64
• **Benchmark 3.** Knows that an organism's patterns of behavior are related to the nature of that organism's environment (e.g., physical characteristics of the environment)	25–28

Standards Correlation Chart *(cont.)*

Standards and Benchmarks	Pages
Science *(cont.)*	
Standard 9. Understand the sources and properties of energy	
• **Benchmark 4.** Knows that light can be reflected, refracted, or absorbed	29–32
Standard 11. Understands the nature of scientific knowledge	
• **Benchmark 3.** Knows that scientists make the results of their investigations public; they describe the investigations in ways that enable others to repeat the investigations	21–24
• **Benchmark 4.** Knows that scientists review and ask questions about the results of other scientists' work	21–24
Standard 13. Understands the scientific enterprise	
• **Benchmark 1.** Knows that people of all ages, backgrounds, and groups have made contributions to science and technology throughout history	21–24
History	
Standard 2. Understands the history of a local community and how communities in North America varied long ago	
• **Benchmark 2.** Knows geographical settings, economic activities, food, clothing, homes, crafts, and rituals of Native American societies long ago (e.g., Iroquois, Sioux, Hopi, Nez Perce, Pueblo, Inuit, Cherokee)	33–36
Standard 4. Understands how democratic values came to be, and how they have been exemplified by people, events, and symbols	
• **Benchmark 3.** Understands how people over the last 200 years have continued to struggle to bring all groups in American society the liberties and equality promised in the basic principles of American democracy	41–44
• **Benchmark 8.** Understands the historical events and democratic values commemorated by major national holidays (e.g., Presidents' Day, Memorial Day)	45–48
• **Benchmark 10.** Knows the Pledge of Allegiance and patriotic songs, poems, and sayings that were written long ago, and understands their significance	37–40
Geography	
Standard 2. Knows the location of places, geographic features, and patterns of the environment	
• **Benchmark 3.** Knows the approximate location of major continents, mountain ranges, and bodies of water on Earth	53–56
Standard 7. Knows the physical processes that shape patterns on Earth's surface	
• **Benchmark 1.** Knows the physical components of Earth's atmosphere (e.g., weather and climate), lithosphere (e.g., land forms such as mountains, hills, plateaus, plains), hydrosphere (e.g., oceans, lakes, rivers), and biosphere (e.g., vegetation and biomes)	57–60
• **Benchmark 3.** Knows how Earth's position relative to the Sun affects events and conditions on Earth (e.g., how the tilt of the Earth in relation to the Sun explains seasons in different locations on Earth, how the length of day influences human activity in different regions of the world)	49–52
Standard 8. Understands the characteristics of ecosystems on Earth's surface	
• **Benchmark 1.** Knows the components of ecosystems at a variety of scales (e.g., fungi, insects, plants, and animals in a food chain or food web; fish and marine vegetation in coastal zones; grasses, birds, and insects in grassland areas)	61–64

Standards Correlation Chart *(cont.)*

Standards and Benchmarks	Pages
Language Arts	
Standard 1. Uses the general skills and strategies of the writing process	
Benchmark 1. Uses prewriting strategies to plan written work (e.g., uses graphic organizers, takes notes, organizes information)	77–80, 89–96
Benchmark 2. Uses strategies to draft and revise written work (elaborates on a central idea; uses paragraphs to develop separate ideas; produces multiple drafts)	89–92
Benchmark 3. Uses strategies to edit and publish written work	81–84, 89–92
Benchmark 4. Evaluates own and others' writing	81–84, 89–92
Benchmark 7. Writes expository compositions (e.g., stays on the topic, develops the topic with simple facts, details, examples and explanation, excludes extraneous information)	81–84
Benchmark 9. Writes autobiographical compositions	89–92
Standard 3. Uses grammatical and mechanical conventions in written compositions	
Benchmark 4. Uses nouns in written compositions	85–88
Benchmark 7. Uses adverbs in written compositions	85–88
Benchmark 10. Uses conventions of spelling in written compositions (e.g., uses compounds, roots, suffixes, prefixes, and syllable constructions to spell words)	85–88
Standard 5. Uses the general skills and strategies of the reading process	
Benchmark 3. Represents concrete information (e.g., persons, places, things, events) as explicit mental pictures	65–68
Benchmark 7. Uses word reference materials (glossary, dictionary, thesaurus) to determine the meaning, pronunciation, and derivations of unknown words	73–76
Standard 6. Uses reading skills and strategies to understand and interpret a variety of literary texts	
Benchmark 1 Uses reading skills and strategies to understand a variety of literary passages and texts (e.g., fables, poems, fairy tales, etc.)	65–72
Benchmark 2. Knows the defining characteristics of a variety of literary forms and genre	69–72
Benchmark 8. Understands the ways in which language is used in literary texts (e.g., personification, alliteration, onomatopoeia, simile, metaphor, imagery, hyperbole, beat, rhythm)	25–28, 73–76
Standard 7. Uses reading skills and strategies to understand and interpret a variety of informational texts	
Benchmark 4. Uses the various parts of a book (e.g., index, table of contents, glossary, appendix, preface) to locate information	77–80
Benchmark 5. Summarizes and paraphrases information in texts (e.g., includes the main idea and significant supporting details of a reading selection)	77–80
Benchmark 6. Uses prior knowledge and experience to understand and respond to new information	77–80

Standards and benchmarks used with permission from McREL.

Copyright 2006 McREL. Mid-continent Research for Education and Learning.

2250 S. Parker Road, Suite 500, Aurora, CO 80014

Telephone: 303-337-0990. Website: *www.mcrel.org/standards-benchmarks.*

Math

Day 1

1. Prior to this lesson, your students must know odd and even numbers and multiplication and division of factors 0–10; and they must have a basic understanding of money (e.g., 10 nickels equals 50 cents, half a dollar is 50 cents).

2. Make an overhead transparency and copies of the "Laying Tiles" organizer on page 10. Obtain clear number tiles (or cut out the ones on your transparency) to use on the overhead.

3. Have your students cut out the individual number tiles on the page.

4. Have your students glue their tile boards to a piece of poster board and store their number tiles in a zipper bag.

5. Tell the students to place the tiles, moving from top to bottom. Working as a class, solve the first two problems. Then have one student come up and display the correct answer on the overhead.

6. Say, "Now we are going to use each tile once. I will ask the question, and you will place the tiles. Do not shout out the answer. If you don't know one, skip it. We'll go over it."

7. Ask these questions: How many eggs are in a dozen? (*12*) How many days in 7 weeks? (*49*) What odd number is a factor of 6? (*3*) How many cents in half a dollar? (*50¢*) What is 42 divided by 6? (*7*) What is the even number between 66 and 70? (*68*) The answers to these problems are shown on the completed graphic organizer on page 9.

8. Go over the answers, asking individual students to explain how they determined the right answer.

Day 2

1. Have students get out their tile boards and number tiles.

2. Ask these questions: What is 48 divided by 8? (*6*) How many hours are in a day? (*24*) I have three quarters. How many cents do I have? (*75¢*) In counting, after the number one, what is the next odd number? (*3*) What is the value of nine dimes? (*90¢*) Name an odd number that is the product of 9. (*81—can't be 18 because that's an even number product of 9*)

Days 3–5

1. Have students get out their tile boards and number tiles.

2. Repeat the activity above using a variety of questions you have prepared in advance.

Next Week

1. Have students get out their tile boards and number tiles.

2. Pair the students. They must place all 10 digits in any order and then write appropriate number sentences or questions next to each number. This is challenging because the children must generate the questions and can use each digit only once.

3. Have each pair write their number sentences and answers on a piece of paper to turn in.

4. If your class enjoys this activity, you can eventually have them do it independently.

Note: This is filled in with the answers to the set of clues given in #7 on page 8.

Math

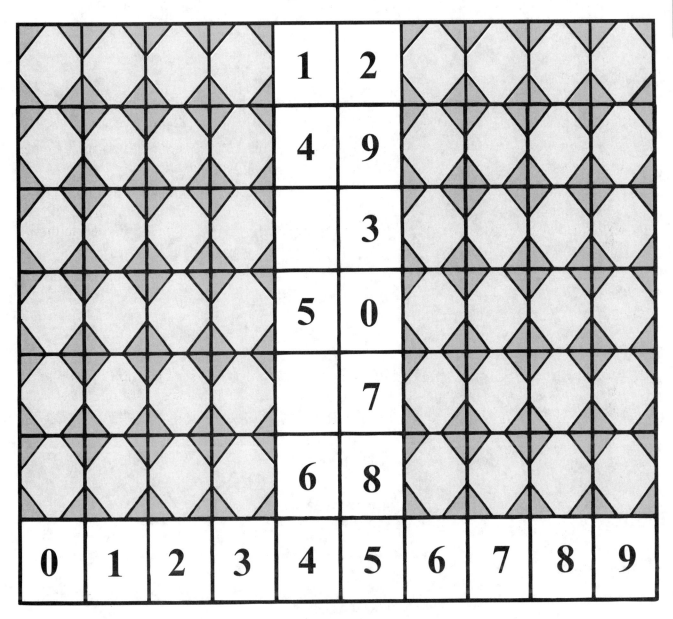

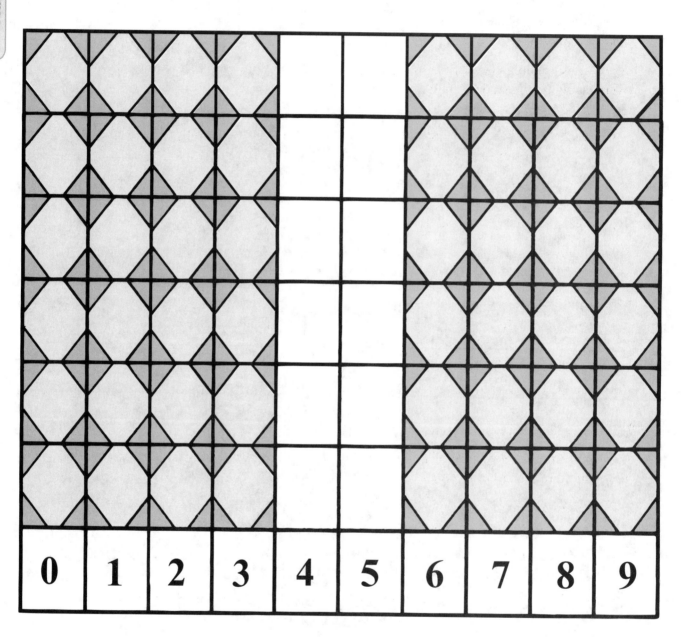

Day 1

1. Prior to this lesson, your students must be familiar with multiplication and division facts up to 12.

2. Make an overhead transparency and two copies for each student of the "Follow the Steps" graphic organizer on page 13.

3. Write this word problem at the top of your transparency:

> *Jenna is buying flowers. Her mom wants to have 4 rows. Each row will have 9 flowers. How many flowers must Jenna buy?*

4. Working as a whole class, solve the problem step by step, filling in the transparency on the overhead while the students do so at their seats.
   - Step 1: 4 rows of 9 flowers. How many total?
   - Step 2: "Of" is a clue word in word problems. It means to multiply. We need 4 groups of 9 flowers. 4 x 9 = total flowers
   - Step 3: 4 x 9 = 36 flowers
   - Step 4: 36 ÷ 9 flowers = 4 rows OR 36 ÷ 4 rows = 9 flowers (the numbers we started with)

5. Wipe clean the transparency and then solve this problem as a class:

> *Jenna bought the 36 flowers. Then her mom decided that she wanted just 3 rows. How many flowers must Jenna put in each row?*

   - Step 1: There are 36 flowers and 3 rows. How many flowers in each row?
   - *Step 2:* Split 36 into 3 equal groups. This means you must divide. 36 ÷ 3 = number of flowers in each row
   - Step 3: 36 ÷ 3 = 12 flowers
   - Step 4: 12 x 3 = 36 flowers (the total we started with)

Day 2

1. Distribute another copy of the "Follow the Steps" graphic organizer to students. Write this problem on the board or overhead and have the students do it independently:

> *Ricky has six friends at his party. He has 21 candy bars. What is the only fair way to split them up evenly? Remember to include Ricky.*

   - Step 1: Ricky has 21 candy bars. Six friends + Ricky = 7 kids. How do you split them up evenly?
   - Step 2: You need to split 21 candy bars into 7 equal groups. You must divide. 21 ÷ 7 = number of candy bars to give each child
   - Step 3: 21 ÷ 7 = 3 candy bars each
   - Step 4: 7 kids x 3 candy bars = 21 candy bars (amount Ricky started with)

2. Collect the students' completed graphic organizers and check for understanding.

3. You can use this graphic organizer for each word problem the students do until they have the steps memorized.

Note: The "Follow the Steps" graphic organizer can be used as a sequencing organizer in any subject area if you cover the words on the steps and in the boxes before you make copies.

Note: This is filled in with the third example from page 11.

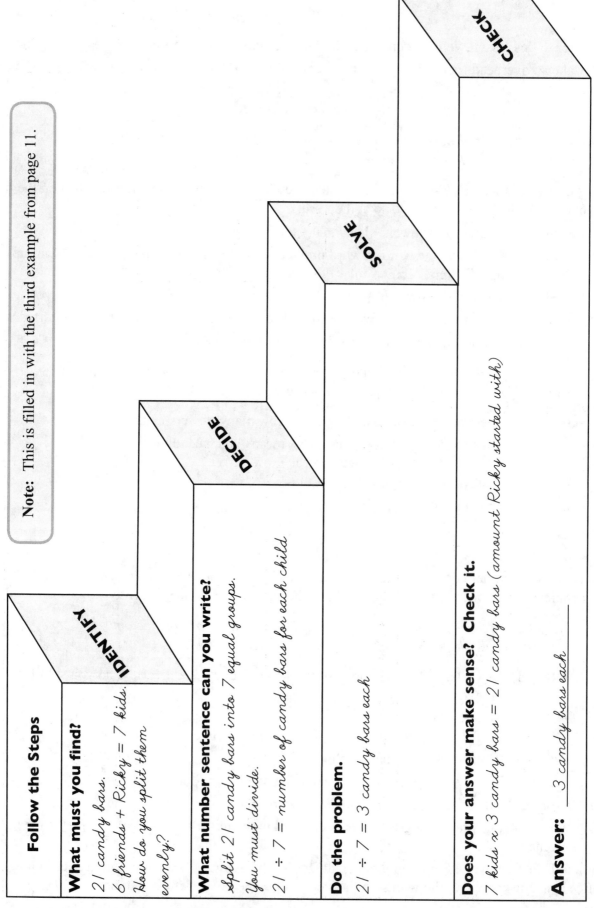

Follow the Steps

What must you find?

21 candy bars.
6 friends + Ricky = 7 kids.
How do you split them evenly?

IDENTIFY

What number sentence can you write?

Split 21 candy bars into 7 equal groups.
You must divide.

21 ÷ 7 = number of candy bars for each child

DECIDE

Do the problem.

21 ÷ 7 = 3 candy bars each

SOLVE

Does your answer make sense? Check it.

7 kids × 3 candy bars = 21 candy bars (amount Ricky started with)

CHECK

Answer: _3 candy bars each_

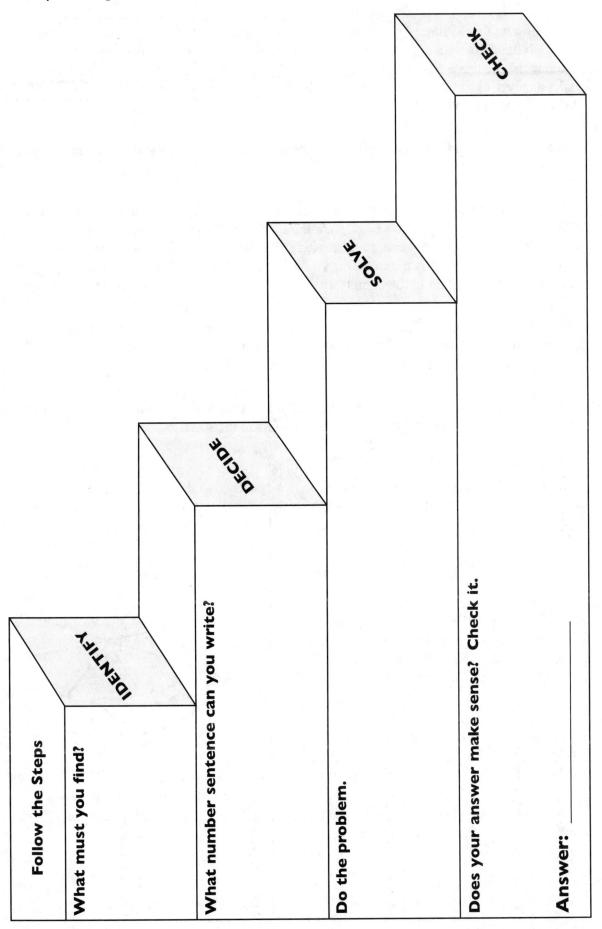

Follow the Steps

What must you find?

IDENTIFY

What number sentence can you write?

DECIDE

Do the problem.

SOLVE

Does your answer make sense? Check it.

CHECK

Answer: _____

1. Prior to doing this lesson, your students should be familiar with addition and subtraction of two-digit numbers with regrouping and basic multiplication and division facts. They should also understand that a fraction shows division. This lesson is intended to solidify your students' understanding of basic math facts, as well the associative and commutative properties of addition. It also serves to provide a link to simple word problems.

2. Make an overhead transparency and student copies of the "It's All Relative" graphic organizer on page 16.

3. Distribute the copies and display the transparency. Write "36 + 57" in the "Expression" column while the students do so at their seats. Ask the students to explain what it means (36 plus 57 more) and other ways that it can be expressed (57 + 36 or 93). Challenge them to come up with a real-life example. One is provided for you in the completed graphic organizer on page 15. You can offer the information in the completed graphic organizer whenever the class is stumped.

4. For the second row, write "78 take away an unknown number will equal 46" in the "What It Means" column. Have the students provide the information for the rest of the columns. You will probably need to help the most with generating the real-life example.

5. For the third row, write "6 groups of 9" in the "What It Means" column and ask the students to volunteer the information for the rest of the columns in the row.

6. In the fourth row, write in the "Real-Life Example" column, "A mom had 48 strawberries and 6 children. She wanted to divide the strawberries equally." Ask the students to volunteer the information for the rest of the columns in the row. They also need to complete the "Real-Life Example."

7. For the fifth row, write, "A pie was cut into eight slices. Then people ate 6/8 of the pie" in the "Real-Life Example" column. Guide your students to fill in the rest of the columns. Ask them how many pie slices are left. Be sure to take time to clear up misconceptions that you may discover when the students volunteer answers.

8. For the sixth row, write "97 − 23 − 17" in the "Can Also Be Expressed As" box. Ask your students if they will get the same answer if they express it as "97 − 17 − 23." Then ask if they will get the same number if they use "17 − 23 − 97" or "23 − 17 − 97." Lead them to draw the conclusion that with subtraction, the largest number needs to appear first but that the smaller numbers can then be subtracted in any order. Ask your students to fill in the rest of the columns.

Math

Expression	What It Means	Can Also Be Expressed As	Real-Life Example
36 + 57	36 plus 57 OR 36 and 57 combined	57 + 36 OR 93	There were 36 pieces in the bubblegum machine. A man added 57 pieces to fill it up. There were 93 pieces in the bubblegum machine when it was full.
78 − ? = 46	78 take away an unknown number will equal 46	78 − 46 = ? OR 32	There were 78 students in the band. After the concert, some went home right away, so just 46 went to the reception. That means that 32 band members went home before the reception.
6 x 9	6 groups of 9	9 x 6 OR 54	Mr. Allen had to buy socks for the kids on the baseball team. He bought 9 packages. Each package had 6 socks. He bought a total of 54 socks for the team.
48 ÷ 6	48 divided by 6 OR 48 split into 6 equal groups	$\frac{48}{6}$ OR 8	A mom had 48 strawberries and 6 children. She wanted to divide them equally, so she gave 8 to each child.
$\frac{6}{8}$	6 out of 8 parts	6 divided by 8 OR $\frac{3}{4}$	A pie was cut into 8 slices. Then people ate 6/8 of the pie. (Two pieces are left.)
97 − 17 − 23	97 minus 17 and then minus 23	97 − 23 − 17 OR 57	There were 97 candles in the box. Cindy put 23 in holders. Then she noticed that more candles were needed. She took another 17 from the box. Then there were 57 candles left in the box.

Math

Expression	What It Means	Can Also Be Expressed As	Real-Life Example

Day 1

1. Bring in some rocks. They can be any type, but some variety would be nice. Display them in a location where the students can see them. Ask your class, "What do you know about rocks? Are rocks alive? Can rocks change?"

2. Make and distribute student copies of "The Rock Cycle" on page 18.

3. Have your class look at the article and identify the words in boldface. Make a list of these words on the board or overhead:

   ✧ **crust**—the hard outer layer of Earth on which we live

   ✧ **molten**—melted

   ✧ **mantle**—the fluid rock layer below Earth's crust

   ✧ **core**—the innermost part of Earth; center of the planet

   ✧ **erode**—gradually wear away

   ✧ **erupts**—spews rocks, gases, and lava

   ✧ **lava**—hot, liquid rock that pours from an erupting volcano

4. Explain, "Often key terms are written in boldface print. These are essential vocabulary words. So, when you see boldface words, pay attention to them. The author is letting you know they are important."

5. Ask your students if they can define any of the boldface words and write the definition after each word on the board or overhead. Supply the definition (see above) of any of the terms that are new to your class.

6. The article is written at 3.2 reading level, so depending upon the needs of your class, you can read it as a whole group, in partners, or independently.

7. Discuss the article.

Day 2

1. Make an overhead transparency and student copies of the "Tire Cycle" graphic organizer on page 20.

2. Display the transparency. Explain that just as a tire on a bike or vehicle goes around and around, so do the seasons in a year. Ask your class to name the seasons in order. Fill in the graphic organizer. Note that there's an order to the seasons (spring has to come before fall), but that you can start with any season; there is no absolute "first."

3. Have your students take out "The Rock Cycle" passage they read yesterday.

4. Wipe the transparency clean. Distribute the student copies of the graphic organizer. Draw the analogy between tires moving around and around and rocks going through the rock cycle repeatedly. The major difference is that a tire goes around rapidly and rocks take thousands or even millions of years to go through their cycle.

5. Have your students refer to the passage to identify the four steps in the rock cycle.

6. Fill in the graphic organizer as a class.

The Rock Cycle

Earth's top rock layer is the **crust**. The crust is broken into huge pieces, like a cracked eggshell. These huge pieces fit together like a jigsaw puzzle. They float on a layer of **molten** rock called the **mantle**. This layer is a thick, hot fluid. It melted due to the weight and pressure of Earth's heavy crust. Earth's center has a solid **core** of cobalt, iron, and nickel. Earth's crust and mantle change over time. But its core does not change.

Even though we cannot see it, rocks are always changing. It happens slowly. The rocks on Earth's surface **erode**. Rain, ice, wind, and moving water make little pieces break off. These little pieces blow away or get carried away by water. When the pieces drop, they form a new layer at the bottom of lakes, rivers, or seas. Like the blankets on a bed, there are many layers. The top layers are the newest. The bottom layers are the oldest. As the layers press down, these rocks harden and get thicker.

After a long, long time, heat and pressure squeeze the lowest layer. All the rock layers above it are heavy! So the lowest rock layer gets hotter and hotter. The rocks start to change. They melt and become part of Earth's mantle. When a volcano **erupts**, they come back to Earth's crust. They flow onto the surface as **lava**. Then the lava cools and hardens. The rocks are solid again. Then the rock cycle starts over.

The Rock Cycle

Wind and water erode rocks on Earth's crust.

Pieces are carried away and drop to the bottom of rivers and lakes to form a new layer.

The liquid rock returns to Earth's surface as lava and then cools and hardens into solid rocks.

The lowest layer is under high heat and pressure; it melts into liquid rock.

Science

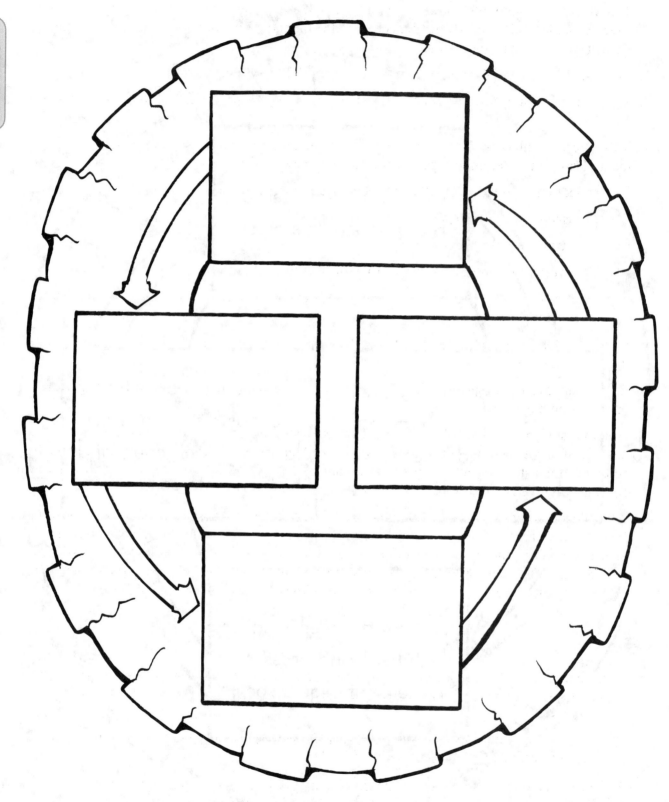

Day 1

1. This would be a good introduction to a unit about fossils or dinosaurs. Before doing this lesson, have available books, encyclopedias, access to the Internet, and other reference materials for students to investigate dinosaurs.

2. Make student copies of "Dinosaur Fossils" on page 22.

3. Make an overhead transparency and student copies of the "K-W-L Chart" graphic organizer on page 24.

4. Write the vocabulary words on the board. See if your students know the definition of any of them. Provide the definitions for any they do not know.

   ✧ **collectors**—people who gather a specific type of thing into a collection

   ✧ **exposed**—able to be seen

   ✧ **scientific**—related to science

   ✧ **discovery**—the process of discovering, or finding

   ✧ **iguana**—a large, green lizard that has a ridge down its spine and can grow to more than five feet in length

5. Distribute the copies of the article. It is written at a 3.8 reading level, so it may be best to read it as a whole class.

6. Display the overhead transparency and distribute student copies of the "K-W-L Chart" graphic organizer on page 24.

7. Ask your students to identify facts that they know about the specific dinosaurs mentioned in the passage. Do not have them write about Anning or Mantell. Use the information to fill in the first column. If the students give incorrect information for the "I Know" column, do not write it down. Explain why it is incorrect.

8. Ask students what they wonder about the six different kinds of dinosaurs mentioned in the article. Write at least three of their questions on the transparency. Each member of the class has the choice to research those questions or questions of his or her choice (as long as three questions are researched). The questions must not be answerable with "yes," "no," names, dates, or numbers. Explain that they are to write the answers in the third column of the graphic organizer.

Days 2–3

1. Give your students time to investigate the books and other materials you gathered prior to the lesson. Depending on the complexity of the questions, you may need to give them time over several days.

2. Create a large K-W-L chart on a piece of poster board. List the questions posed by the class (from the "K-W-L Chart" transparency).

3. Reconvene as a whole group. Ask volunteers to provide the answers and write them across from the questions on the chart. Have students who pursued their own questions offer what they learned and add it to the class chart. Keep the class K-W-L chart on display throughout the unit.

Science

Dinosaur Fossils

Did you know that a 13-year-old girl found the first dinosaur fossil? Mary Anning lived in England near the sea coast. Mary's dad took her and her brother Joe to hunt for fossils. Fossils are ancient animals and plants that have turned into rocks over time. The family searched the sea cliffs. They dug out small fossils. They cleaned them. They put them on their front porch. Collectors bought them. When Mary was 11 years old, her dad died. Still, the children kept finding and selling fossils. One day, she and Joe dug out a big head. They could not find its body. But they were thrilled. They had never seen anything like it.

A big storm hit in 1812. Wind and waves knocked rocks from the cliffs. The rest of the skeleton was exposed! Mary saw it. It was 20 feet long. She did not know it, but she had just found the first dinosaur. Years later, scientists named it *Ichthyosaur*. It swam in the sea millions of years ago.

In 1823 Mary found a nearly complete Plesiosaurus skeleton. Five years later, she found the first fossil of a flying dinosaur. It was a Pterosaur. People bought these fossils. They studied them. Then they put them in museums.

Mary never wrote about her findings. So, few books today give her credit for discovering dinosaurs. The credit goes to Gideon Mantell. Why? When a person makes a scientific discovery, he or she must tell others about it. Then other scientists can study the findings. This means that the person who writes about a discovery gets the credit.

How did Mantell get involved? In 1822 his wife saw teeth sticking out of a rock. She showed it to him. He knew that it was a fossil. But he did not know what the animal was. Mantell took the rock home. He studied it. The rock around the teeth was 130 million years old. He looked at animal skeletons. He wanted to find a match. In 1824 he saw that the teeth looked like an iguana's. So Mantell wrote an article. He called the animal *Iguanadon*. He stated that huge lizards had once walked on Earth.

Nine years later, a whole Iguanadon skeleton was found. Mantell spent months piecing it together. Then he wrote more articles about dinosaurs. He told about their teeth. Those with flat teeth, like the Stegosaurus, ate plants. Those with pointed teeth, like the Tyrannosaurus Rex, ate animals. Mantell also stated that all dinosaurs were reptiles and laid eggs.

K-W-L Chart

I Know

- Ichthyosaur was a sea dinosaur millions of years ago.
- In 1823 a Plesiosaurus was found.
- A Pterosaur was a flying dinosaur.
- In 1833 a complete Iguanadon skeleton was found.
- A Stegosaurus had flat teeth and ate plants.
- A Tyrannosaurus Rex had sharp teeth and ate other animals

I Wonder

- Was the Pterosaur the first bird?
- What did the Stegosaurus look like?
- How many teeth did a Tyrannosaurus Rex have?
- What was a Tyrannosaurus Rex's teeth like?

I Learned

- The Pterosaur was not the first bird. In fact, Pterosaurs are not closely related to either birds or bats. They were a separate species that did not evolve into anything else and died out completely.
- The Stegosaurus had a small, pointed head, bony plates on its back, and spikes on its tail to protect it from predators.
- The T-Rex had 50–60 teeth.
- Some were 11" long and weighed a pound each! Others were just an inch long. All were razor-sharp. The T-Rex grew new teeth often.

Science

K-W-L Chart

I Learned

I Wonder

I Know

1. This lesson is good to use to introduce or wrap up a unit on animal adaptations. The poem talks about hibernation and eating what's available. The graphic organizer will be filled in based on discussion of these and other animal adaptations.

2. Make studen   25t copies of the poem "The Wood Mouse" on page 26. Introduce any unfamiliar vocabulary:

    ✧ **ode**—a lyric poem with irregular metrical form that expresses enthusiastic emotion

    ✧ **'tis**—archaic contraction of "it is"

    ✧ **spring**—place where water bubbles up from the ground

    ✧ **timid**—shy

    ✧ **seldom**—not often; rarely

    ✧ **wiry**—thin; lean

    ✧ **secure**—safe

    ✧ **dreary**—depressing; dismal; sorrowful

    ✧ **boughs**—tree limbs

3. Distribute the copies and read the poem aloud to the class. Then, have the class reread it chorally.

4. Explain that a British woman wrote this poem about field mice, one of the most common mammals of Europe and Asia. In addition to grassy fields, they live in woods, and forests. Often people call the ones that live among trees "wood mice."

5. Reread to your class the fourth and fifth stanzas. Ask, "What animal adaptation is the poet talking about?" (*hibernation*) "Why do animals hibernate?" (*It's too cold for them to be out in the winter; there's no food for them to find in the winter; they would be easy prey against the white backdrop of snow; etc.*) "What do animals that cannot hibernate do to escape winter?" (*They migrate.*) Explain that hibernation and migration are behaviors that help the animals to survive.

6. Make an overhead transparency and student copies of the organizer on page 28.

7. Display the transparency and distribute the student copies. Have the students fill in the graphic organizers at their seats as you do so on the overhead.

8. Say, "Hibernation and migration are animal adaptations. These behaviors increase their chance of survival. What are some other animal adaptations?" (*Answers include body features (wings, claws, fat layer, etc.), appearance (camouflage coloring, stripes, spots, etc.), movement (crawl, fly, freeze in place, etc.), food (eat what's available), etc.*) Discuss each adaptation thoroughly.

9. Ask your students to state the main idea of what you are discussing and write it on the umbrella's handle. (*Answer: Animals' adaptations help them to survive in their environment.*)

10. Ask students to volunteer kinds of adaptations and write each one on a section of the umbrella. (*See completed graphic organizer on page 27.*) Encourage your students to include examples of animals for each section.

Note: You may want to add the behavioral adaptation of *aestivation* (*ehs tuh VAY shuhn*)—a dormant state that some animals have during hot, dry periods. Mention animals (*such as desert lizards*) that use this adaptation during the hottest season in a desert or tropical environment. Lungfish in streams that dry up during the hot season in Africa do this, too.

Science

The Wood Mouse
by Mary Howitt

Do you know the little Wood-Mouse
That pretty little thing,
That sits among the forest leaves,
Beside the forest spring?

Its fur is red as the red chestnut,
And it is small and slim
It leads a life most innocent
Within the forest dim.

'Tis a timid, gentle creature,
And seldom comes in sight
It has a long and wiry tail,
And eyes both black and bright.

It makes its nest of soft, dry moss,
In a hole so deep and strong
And there it sleeps secure and warm,
The dreary winter long.

And though it keeps no calendar,
It knows when flowers are springing
And wakens to its summer life
When Nightingales are singing.

Upon the boughs the Squirrel sits,
The Wood-Mouse plays below
And plenty of food it finds itself
Where the Beech and Chestnut grow.

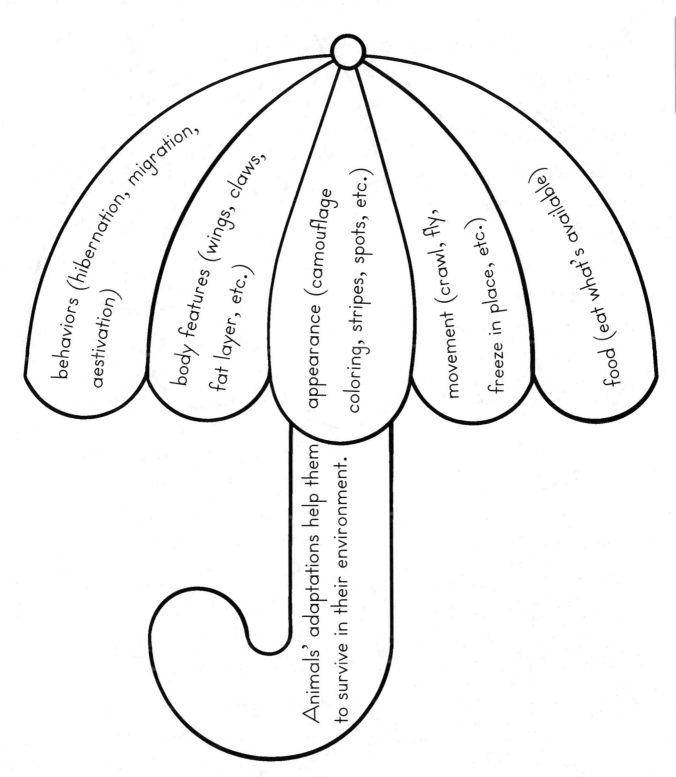

behaviors (hibernation, migration, aestivation)

body features (wings, claws, fat layer, etc.)

appearance (camouflage coloring, stripes, spots, etc.)

movement (crawl, fly, freeze in place, etc.)

food (eat what's available)

Animals' adaptations help them to survive in their environment.

Science

Science

Day 1

1. This is a good introductory lesson about light. Have ready a ball (*any solid color*); a mirror; a tall, clear glass of water with a straw in it; and a pair of sunglasses.

2. Make student copies of "Understanding Light" on page 30. Introduce unfamiliar vocabulary:

   ✧ **overcast**—the condition of the sky when more than 95% is covered by clouds

   ✧ **absorb**—take in; soak up

   ✧ **opaque**—not transparent; not allowing light to pass through

   ✧ **polished**—smooth, shiny, glossy

   ✧ **refract**— deflect in a change of direction

   ✧ **imaginary**—pretend; not real

3. This article is written at a 3.5 reading level, so depending upon the needs of your class, you can have the students read it as a whole group, as partners, or independently.

4. Show your students the ball. Ask what property of light it displays. (*that light enables us to see; that an opaque object absorbs all light except its own color*)

5. Show your students the mirror. Ask what property of light it displays. (*that light enables us to see; that light reflects; that light reflects best from a flat, shiny surface*)

6. Show your students the glass of water with the straw. Ask what property of light it displays. (*that light enables us to see; that light refracts (bends) as it moves through different substances*) Be sure that your students each get to see the refraction of the straw. Remove the straw to prove that it is actually straight.

7. Show your students the sunglasses. Ask what property of light the glasses display. (*that light enables us to see; we get light from the sun; sunlight gets through clouds even on overcast days; light reflects off snow and ice, so we still need sunglasses in winter.*)

Day 2

1. Have the students reread the article "Understanding Light."

2. Make an overhead transparency and student copies of the "Key Points" graphic organizer on page 32.

3. Display the transparency and distribute the student copies.

4. Explain that you are going to summarize the key points from each paragraph in the article. The main idea of the paragraph goes in the center of the key ring. The key points about the main idea go at the end of each key on the ring.

5. As a class, read the first paragraph. Discuss the main idea. The main idea is not stated in the first paragraph and must be constructed from a combination of the ideas given.

6. As a class, determine three key points that support the main idea of the first paragraph.

7. In the second, third, and fourth paragraphs, the main idea is stated in the first sentence. However, the key points need to be extrapolated.

8. Fill in the graphic organizer as a class, while the students do so at their seats.

Science

Understanding Light

The sun gives us light each day. Even on a dark, cloudy day, some of the sun's rays reach us. That's why when it is overcast it is not as dark as night. Sunlight looks like it has no color. But it contains all colors. We know this because a rainbow forms when water drops in the air break sunlight into its different colors. A rainbow has streaks of red, orange, yellow, green, blue, indigo, and violet. Each time that you see a rainbow, the colors will be in this order. The pattern is always the same.

Light can be absorbed. That is how we see colors. Opaque things absorb all colors except for their own color. For example, when light rays fall on a blue box, it looks blue. Why? Its surface absorbs all the other colors except blue.

Light can be reflected. When light rays hit any surface, they bounce off it. The surface reflects the light. When light reflects from a smooth surface, all of its rays reflect in the same direction. When light reflects from a rough surface, the rays reflect in many directions. So flat, shiny things reflect light the best. Think about your bathroom mirror. It is a flat sheet of polished glass with a shiny silver coating on its back. Light reflects off snow and ice, too. That's why you need sunglasses on a sunny day in winter.

Light can be refracted. Light moves at different speeds through different substances. It moves faster through air than through water or glass. When light rays slow down, they change direction slightly. They refract. This makes the light rays appear to bend at the spot where two substances meet. This is why a straight straw in a glass of water does not look straight. When you look at the straw through the glass, the straw seems to bend. That's because light moves through both the glass and the water at different speeds. On a hot day, refraction makes you see imaginary puddles on the road ahead even when the pavement is dry. Why? Light moving through cool air changes speed as it enters the hot air near the road's surface. The light seems to "bend." Refracting makes the air shine. So it looks like water shimmering in the sun. But there is nothing there. That's why when you get closer, the image disappears.

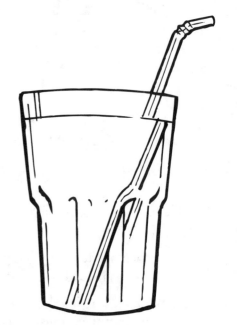

Sunlight reaches us even on overcast days, and its light contains all colors. Some of the sun's rays shine through clouds. A rainbow is sunlight broken into its colors.

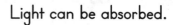

Light can be absorbed. This is why we can see colors. Opaque things absorb all the colors but their own. A green plant looks green because its leaves absorb all colors but green.

Light can be reflected. When light hits any surface, it bounces off. Flat, shiny things reflect light the best. Rough surfaces reflect light in many directions.

Light can be refracted. Light moves at different speeds through different substances. When light rays slow down, they change direction slightly (refract). Light moving from cool to hot air refracts. This causes imaginary puddles to appear on the road.

Science

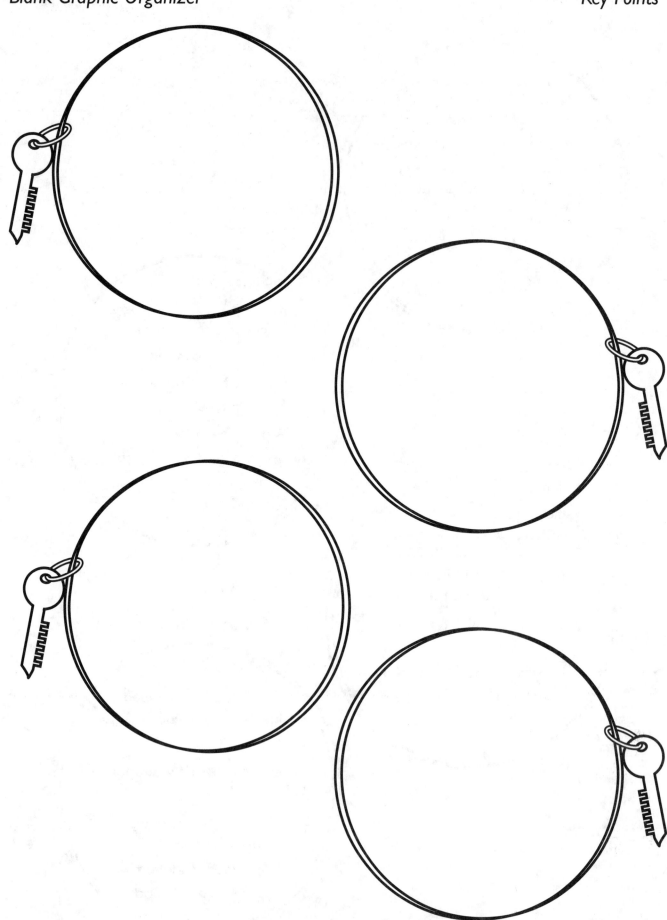

Day 1

1. This lesson is a good introduction to these two prominent Native-American cultures.

2. On a map, point out the territory in the central part of New York state (Finger Lakes region) where the Iroquois (eer-UH-kwoi) lived. The Iroquois were an important Native-American confederacy also called the Five Nations, comprised of the Mohawk, Oneida, Onondaga, Cayuga, and Seneca (and later the Tuscarora) tribes. This was the first democracy in North America.

3. Point out on a map where the Pueblo Indians lived. Their range extended from Mexico through New Mexico, Arizona, Utah, and Colorado.

4. Introduce any unfamiliar vocabulary:

   ✧ **sustains**—provides for; supplies with necessities or nourishment

   ✧ **furnish**—give; provide

   ✧ **embodies** (em-BOD-eez)—represents

   ✧ **garment**—article of clothing

   ✧ **warp**—the yarn held stationary on a loom that intersects at right angles with the weft yarn in woven cloth; the lengthwise threads in woven fabric

   ✧ **weft**—the yarn on a loom that is carried by the shuttle and intersects at right angles with the warp yarn in woven cloth

   ✧ **fittingly**—appropriate; suitable

5. Make and distribute student copies of "In the Native Americans' Own Words" on page 34.

6. Read both poems aloud to your class. Then have the students read each one chorally.

7. Discuss the poems. Ask your students, "How are these Native-American cultures alike? How are they different? How do you know?"

Day 2

1. Make an overhead transparency and student copies of "Venn Diagram" on page 36. Cut out a yellow transparent circle and a blue transparent circle the same size as the circles in the Venn diagram. (You can use a red transparency if you don't have blue.)

2. Display the transparency and demonstrate how a Venn diagram works by placing a yellow transparent circle over one circle. Explain that this circle represents information related to the Iroquois. Remove the yellow circle.

3. Next place a blue transparent circle over the other circle. Explain that this circle represents information related to the Pueblo.

4. Now put the yellow transparent circle back down. The intersection of the two circles is green. Just as the color green is part yellow and part blue, the information in the intersection of the circles is a part of both circles and relates to both tribes. Remove the transparent circles.

5. Distribute the diagram to the students. Have them quietly reread both poems. Ask for information that is relevant to both tribes and write it in the intersection while the students do so at their seats.

6. Have the students discern information that is unique to each culture and write it in the appropriate circle. Complete the Venn diagram on the overhead as the students follow along.

History

In the Native Americans' Own Words

Iroquois Thanksgiving

–an Iroquois prayer

We return thanks to our mother,

the Earth,

which sustains us.

We return thanks to the rivers
   and streams,

which supply our water.

We return thanks to all herbs,

which furnish medicines for the care
   of our ill.

We return thanks to the corn, and to
   her sisters, the beans and squashes,

which give us life.

We return thanks to the bushes
   and trees,

which provide us with fruit.

We return thanks to the wind,

which brings the weather.

We return thanks to the moon
   and stars,

which give us their light when the
   sun is gone.

We return thanks to the sun,

which makes the plants grow.

We return thanks to the Great Spirit,

who embodies all goodness,

and who directs all things for the
   good of His children.

Song of the Sky Loom

–a Pueblo song

Oh, our Mother, the Earth!

Oh, our Father, the Sky!

Your children are we.

And with tired backs

we bring you the gifts that you love.

Then weave for us a garment of
   brightness;

May the warp be the white light
   of morning,

May the weft be the red light
   of evening,

May the fringes be the falling rain,

May the border be the standing
   rainbow.

Thus weave for us a garment of
   brightness;

That we may walk fittingly where
   birds sing,

That we may walk fittingly where
   grass is green.

Oh, our Mother, the Earth!

Oh, our Father, the Sky!

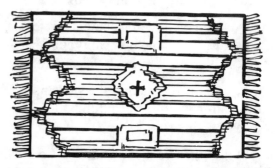

34

The Pueblo

- call the sky "our Father"
- offer gifts to the Earth and the Sky
- want to walk "fittingly" on Earth in relationship with nature

(overlap)
- call Earth "our mother"
- refer to the sun and weather in positive ways
- show deep appreciation and respect for nature

The Iroquois

- offer thanks for the Earth, water, medicine, food, weather, sun, moon, and stars
- believe in the Great Spirit
- offer thanks to the Great Spirit

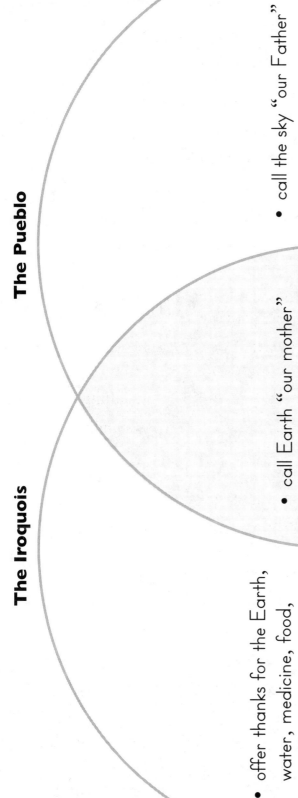

History

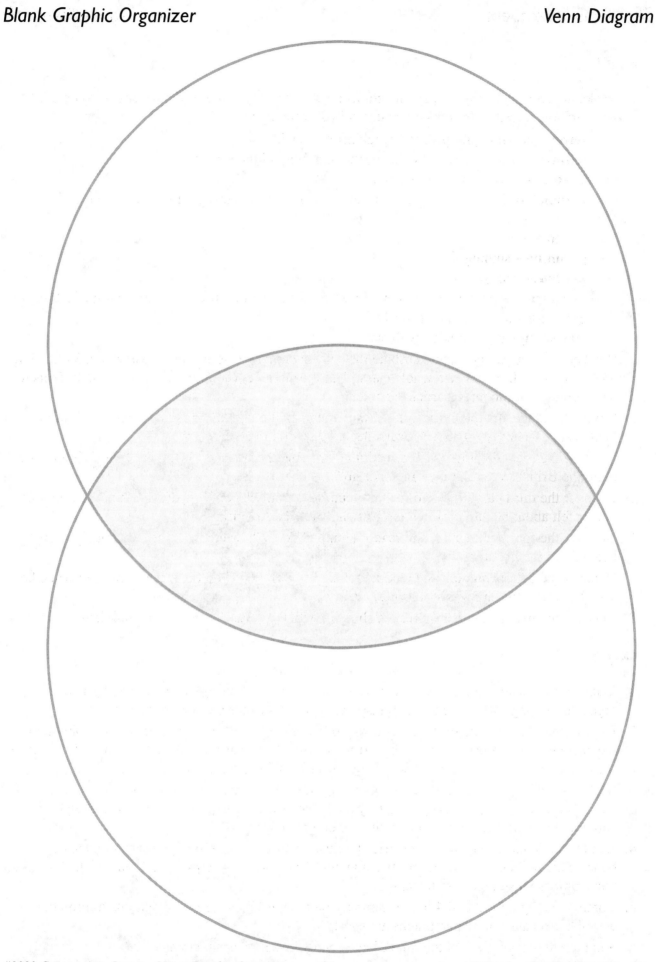

Day 1

1. Make an overhead transparency and student copies of "The Story of the American National Anthem" on page 38. Introduce any unfamiliar vocabulary:
   ✧ **seized**—forcibly grabbed; taken against one's will
   ✧ **enemies**—armed foes; members of the opposing military force
   ✧ **release**—to free from confinement
   ✧ **national anthem**—a song recognized as the formal expression of patriotic feelings about a nation
   ✧ **hailed**—honored
   ✧ **gleaming**—shining
   ✧ **perilous**—dangerous
   ✧ **rampart**—an embankment often topped with a stone wall used for the defense of a fort
   ✧ **gallantly**—bravely, courageously
   ✧ **star-spangled**—sprinkled with stars

2. Display the transparency and distribute the student copies. This article is written at a 3.8 reading level, so you will read it as a whole class. Use a paper to cover all but the title. Ask students to make predictions about the article's content.

3. Cover all but the first paragraph. Read the paragraph aloud to the students as they follow along at their seats. Then say, "The Americans declared war on the British. Why?"

4. Uncover the second paragraph and read it aloud. Ask the students, "Why did Francis Scott Key think the British would let their prisoner go?"

5. Uncover the third paragraph and read it aloud. Ask your class, "How do you think Key and the doctor felt about having to watch the British attack the American fort?"

6. Uncover the fourth paragraph and read it aloud. Ask, "Why were the Americans put in a small boat tied to the big ship?"

7. Uncover the fifth paragraph and read it aloud. Ask, "How do you think the doctor felt when he saw the American flag was still flying? Why?"

8. Uncover the national anthem. Read it chorally with the class. Then, sing it with them.

Day 2

1. Make an overhead transparency and student copies of the "Bare Bones Summary" graphic organizer on page 40. Display the transparency and distribute the student copies.

2. Explain that this graphic organizer is a way of summarizing the most important information in the passage. The information will be written in complete sentences inside the bones. It will be a shortened version of the passage with only the critical ideas included.

3. Reread the passage. Summarize the first paragraph on the first bone. (See the completed graphic organizer on page 39). Explain why Key's mission was not included (it's not the highlight of this paragraph and will be covered in depth in another paragraph).

4. Ask the students to help you summarize the information in the second paragraph on the second bone. This will be challenging for the students. You may want to put their ideas on the board and then compose a summary statement.

5. Combine paragraphs 3 and 4 in the summary on the third bone. Explain that this information is combined because these paragraphs are short.

6. Summarize paragraph 5 on the fourth bone. Sing the national anthem again.

History

The Story of the American National Anthem

Francis Scott Key had a friend who was a prisoner on a British ship. Key and his friend were Americans. The man was a prisoner because the Americans and British were fighting the War of 1812. The war started after the British in Canada gave guns to Native Americans. They encouraged them to kill American settlers. And the British had also seized thousands of American men. They made them join the British Navy! Why? Great Britain was fighting France. They needed more sailors.

Key went to the ship. He brought letters from British soldiers. They were the prisoners of Americans. The letters said that Key's friend was a doctor. He had taken good care of them even though they were enemies. They asked for his release. The men needed his care.

The British said that the doctor could go. But Key and the doctor had to wait. First, the British ship had to attack Fort McHenry in Maryland. They did not want Key and the doctor to warn the Americans. They promised to let them go after the battle ended.

On September 13, 1814, the British attacked. Key and his friend were put in a small boat tied to the ship. They watched the fight. They saw the American flag flying over the fort. The battle raged all day and night. The men tried to see through the smoke. Who was winning?

In the morning, the battle ended. As the smoke cleared, Key saw the American flag. It still flew over the fort. The Americans had won! Key was so happy that he wrote a poem. It was "The Star-Spangled Banner." Later this poem was made into a song. It is our national anthem.

The Star-Spangled Banner
by Francis Scott Key

O say can you see, by the dawn's early light,
What so proudly we hailed at the twilight's last gleaming?
Whose broad stripes and bright stars through the perilous fight
O'er the ramparts we watched were so gallantly streaming!
And the rockets' red glare, the bombs bursting in air,
Gave proof through the night that our flag was still there!
O say does that star-spangled banner yet wave
O'er the land of the free and the home of the brave?

This is the 15-star flag that Key saw flying over Fort McHenry.

Sample Graphic Organizer   **Bare Bones Summary**

The Americans and British fought the War of 1812. The British gave guns to Native Americans to kill American settlers. The British forced American men to join the British Navy to fight France.

Francis Scott Key, an American, went to the British ship where an American doctor was prisoner. He brought letters from imprisoned British soldiers. They asked for the doctor's release.

The British said that the doctor could go after they attacked Fort McHenry in Maryland. Key and the doctor watched the battle. They couldn't tell who was winning.

In the morning, Key saw the American flag at the fort. The Americans had won! Then Key wrote a poem called "The Star-Spangled Banner." It was made into the U.S. national anthem.

History

Day 1

1. Make student copies of "Frederick Douglass: He Stood Up for Others" on page 42. Introduce any unfamiliar vocabulary:

   ❖ **advocate**— a person who speaks or writes in support or defense of another person or a cause

   ❖ **abolitionist**—a person who supported the end of slavery, especially before the U.S. Civil War

   ❖ **trough**—a long, narrow, shallow receptacle used to hold water or feed for animals

   ❖ **mistress**—female slave owner (usually the master's wife)

   ❖ **literacy**—the ability to read and write

   ❖ **autobiography**—the story of a person's life (written by that person)

   ❖ **exposed**—uncovered; made known

   ❖ **editor**—supervisor who oversees the publication of a newspaper, magazine, or books

2. Distribute student copies. This piece is written at a 3.4 reading level, but it would probably be best to read it as a whole class or in partners due to the complexity of ideas.

Day 2

1. Reread the article about Frederick Douglass. Since this is a repeated reading and the children are familiar with the text, have them take turns reading it aloud.

2. Make an overhead transparency and student copies of the "This One Is a Diamond" graphic organizer on page 44.

3. Display the transparency and distribute the student copies.

4. Explain that you are going to summarize the information in the article on the graphic organizer.

5. Fill out the information in the graphic organizer on the overhead while the students do so at their seats. Prompt your students to share their ideas.

6. The completed graphic organizer is shown on page 43, but it does not provide the only possible answers. Use your students' ideas wherever possible so that they "own" the project.

Days 3–5

1. Have available for student use picture books about famous Americans such as George Washington, Abraham Lincoln, Rosa Parks, Martin Luther King, Jr., Susan B. Anthony, etc. The picture books ensure that the students will be able to quickly read and understand the information contained within them.

2. Pair the students. Distribute new student copies of the graphic organizer.

3. Each pair must choose a famous person to write about. Then they must work together to read one or more picture books about the person and complete the graphic organizer about the person.

4. Have the students cut out their diamonds and mount them on construction paper.

5. Let each pair choose one person to share the information with the class.

6. Hang the projects from the ceiling using string or post them in the hallway for other classes to enjoy. This would be a great project to have on display for open house.

History

Frederick Douglass: He Stood Up for Others

Frederick Douglass was a great advocate for African Americans. During the mid 1800s, he was one of the best-known abolitionists in America. But no one knew he would be famous when he was born in 1817. He lived on a farm in Maryland. His mother was a slave, too. She had to work all the time. So Betsey Baily, his grandmother, raised him. He lived with her and rarely saw his mom.

When he turned 6, he had to work as a slave, too. With the other slaves, he was forced to eat cornmeal mush from a pig trough! Later, he was chosen to work in the house. His mistress taught him to read and write. Her husband found out. He got mad and said she must stop. It was against the law to teach a slave. Why? An educated slave would be hard to control. Frederick heard them argue. He saw the value of literacy.

Then he was traded to another farmer. There he was beaten. He dreamed of being free. When he was 13, his grandmother was too old to work. She was thrown out of her cabin and left to die in the woods! Frederick was upset. But he could do nothing to help her. He hated being powerless.

He started teaching other slaves. They had a plot to escape. It was found out, and they were put in jail. A former master rescued Frederick. He put him to work in a shipyard. When he was 21 years old, Frederick made a daring escape north. However, even in New York he was not safe. Slave catchers were always looking for runaways. So Frederick changed his last name from Baily to Douglass. Even so, he was in constant danger. Still, he dared to stand up for others. He knew he had to speak out to help his fellow slaves.

In 1841, Frederick spoke about freedom at the Massachusetts Antislavery Society. The group members liked his speech. They hired him to give speeches about his life as a slave. In 1845, he wrote his autobiography. It exposed the fact that he was a runaway slave. Slave catchers came for him. So he went to England. While there, he spoke out against slavery.

Six years later, Frederick came back to the United States. He started a newspaper called *North Star*. He filled it with articles about the evils of slavery. He made his home a part of the Underground Railroad, too. It was not a railroad with trains. It was hundreds of homes. They belonged to people who fed and hid runaway slaves during the day. Then the runaways moved north at night. Most slaves tried to get to Canada to be safe.

The American Civil War raged from 1861–1865. Frederick helped get African Americans to fight in the Union Army. The war ended slavery. In 1870, Frederick was made the editor of a Washington, D.C., newspaper. He continued to talk and write about equality for all people until his death in 1895.

Frederick
first name

Born 1817

abolitionist, speaker, writer
occupation(s)/character traits

Grandson **of** Betsey Baily
relative **relative**

He loved freedom, the Underground Railroad, and literacy

He felt compassion for others and desire for equality

He feared slave owners and slave catchers

He wanted slavery to end

Lived in Maryland, New York, England, and Washington, D.C.

Died 1895

Douglass
last name

History

_____
first name

Born _____

_____
occupation(s)/character traits

_____ **of** _____
relative **relative**

He loved _____

He felt _____

He feared _____

He wanted _____

Lived in _____

Died _____

_____
last name

Day 1

1. Make an overhead transparency and student copies of "An Important American Holiday" on page 46. Introduce any unfamiliar vocabulary:

   ❖ **slavery**—owning slaves (human beings) and making them do work for free

   ❖ **Confederate States of America**—the new nation formed by the states that left the Union

   ❖ **Northern states (the Union)**—Maine, New Hampshire, Vermont, Massachusetts, Rhode Island, Connecticut, New York, New Jersey, Delaware, and Pennsylvania

   ❖ **Southern states (the Confederacy)**—Virginia, North Carolina, South Carolina, Georgia, Florida, Alabama, Mississippi, Tennessee, Arkansas, Louisiana, and Texas

   ❖ **border states**—states that did not officially declare loyalty to either the Union or the Confederacy (Maryland, West Virginia, Missouri, and Kentucky)

   ❖ **reunited**—put back together again after a separation

   ❖ **tradition**—a belief or custom handed down from one generation to the next

   ❖ **Congress**—the national legislature consisting of the Senate and the House of Representatives

   ❖ **veterans**—people who have served in the armed forces, especially during a war.

2. Display the transparency and distribute the student copies. This article is written at a 3.9 reading level, so you will read it as a whole class. Use a paper to cover all but the title. Ask your students to make predictions about the article's content.

3. Cover all but the first paragraph. Have a student read it aloud as the rest of the class follows along. Then say, "What does the author mean by 'That's why it's called Memorial Day'?"

4. Uncover the second paragraph and read it aloud. Then say, "Name one reason why the American Civil War was fought." Then ask, "What is the other reason? What were the Northern troops called? What were the Southern troops called?"

5. Uncover the third paragraph and read it aloud. Ask, "Why do you think people kept the tradition going?"

6. Uncover the last paragraph. Have a student read it aloud. Ask, "Why do you think Congress made Memorial Day a national holiday? What do you usually do on Memorial Day?"

Day 2

1. Make an overhead transparency and student copies of graphic organizer on page 48. Display the transparency and distribute the copies.

2. Explain that taking notes helps you to remember information you have read. One does this by noting the main idea and important details. Ask what the hair on a horse's neck is called. Explain the play on words and how you will write the main idea on the horse's mane.

3. Have students take out their articles from yesterday and choose individual students to read aloud each paragraph.

4. Ask the class to state the main idea for the whole article. Ask leading questions to guide their response. Write the main idea on the horse's mane while they do so at their seats.

5. Explain that the important details will be written on the horse's body. Have students volunteer details. If students give irrelevant details, gently guide them by saying, "Does that support the main idea?" Complete the graphic organizer as a class.

History

An Important American Holiday

Can you name the holiday that falls on the last Monday of each May? It is a day to remember people who have died in wars. That's why it's called Memorial Day.

Memorial Day started after the American Civil War. In 1861 the U.S. states in the North were against slavery. The U.S. states in the South wanted slavery to be legal. Their way of life was based on free labor. Neither side would back down. Then some of the states in the South left the Union. They said that they were no longer a part of the United States of America. Instead, they formed the Confederate States of America. Abraham Lincoln was the U.S. president. He did not want the nation split in two. So people in the North fought the people in the South.

The Civil War lasted four years. Many men died. In April 1865, the North won. The nation was reunited. But there was still hatred and anger between the North and the South. Then, in 1866 some women showed that they cared about the soldiers who had died. They put flowers on their graves. They did it for men from both sides. They wanted to honor them all. Newspapers wrote about their kind act. People kept the tradition going year after year.

More than 100 years later, Congress passed a law. It made Memorial Day a national holiday. On Memorial Day, we think of the men and women who have died fighting for America. We think about how glad we are to be free. We get a day off from school. There are parades and speeches. People put flowers or flags on veterans' graves.

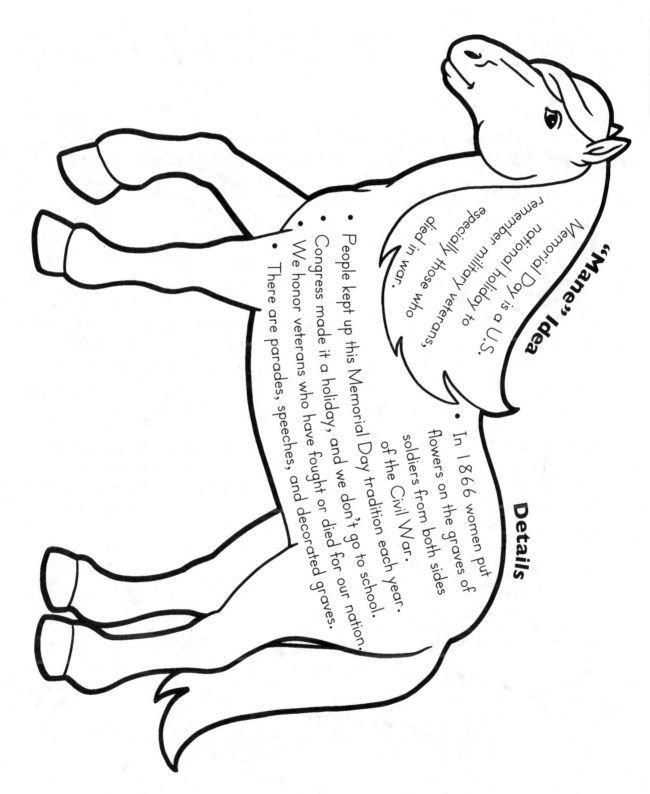

"Mane" Idea

Memorial Day is a U.S. national holiday to remember military veterans, especially those who died in war.

Details

• In 1866 women put flowers on the graves of soldiers from both sides of the Civil War.

• People kept up this Memorial Day tradition each year. Congress made it a holiday, and we don't go to school. We honor veterans who have fought or died for our nation.

• There are parades, speeches, and decorated graves.

History

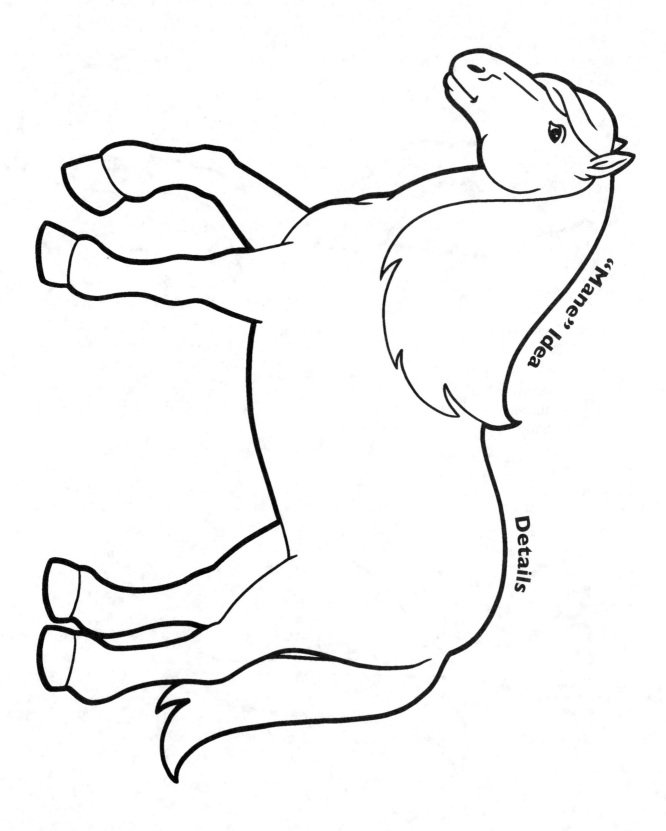

"Mane" Idea

Details

Day 1

1. Make one copy of the "Thinking Guide" graphic organizer on page 52. Write just the boldfaced statements from the completed organizer on page 51 on this copy. Then make and distribute student copies of the "Thinking Guide" graphic organizer with the statements.

2. Distribute the student copies and read aloud the directions and the statements. Pause after each statement to give your students a few moments to write "A" or "D" in the "Me" column. Collect the graphic organizers.

3. Make and distribute copies of the poems on page 50. Introduce unfamiliar vocabulary:
   - ✧ **'round**—abbreviated form of the word "around" to make it one syllable
   - ✧ **eve**—abbreviated form of the word "evening" to make it one syllable
   - ✧ **sleepyhead**—tired child

4. Use "The Sun's Travels" to teach that when it's day on one side of Earth, it is night on the other. Stress that "Indian" in this poem means children from India, not Native Americans.

5. Have your class chorally read "The Sun's Travels" twice. Discuss the poem to be sure that the students understand it. It was written by a man in Great Britain (*show them where this is on a globe*), so the "children in the West" are those in North and South America (*the continents to the west of Europe*).

6. Make the classroom as dark as possible. The darker the room, the better the demonstration. Have a volunteer stand in the front of the room and hold a large flashlight. Explain that this represents the sun, which is always shining.

7. Have another volunteer represent Earth and stand so the flashlight shines on her left side. Pin a sign with the words "Where We Live" to the front of the child. Tell the class to imagine that she is Earth. State, "Notice that her front is partially lighted. This represents sunrise where we live on Earth." Point out that the rest of her body is darkened, and the side opposite the sun is the darkest.

8. Direct the child to turn one-quarter (*90 degrees*) to her left. The sign is now bathed in light. State, "It is now noon on the part of Earth where we live. Notice that the back of her body is darkest. That's because it's midnight on the other side of the world."

9. Have the child turn another one-quarter to her left. Her right side now faces the light. Guide your students to state that this is sunset where you live on Earth.

10. Have the child turn another one-quarter to her left. Her back is now lit up, and the sign is completely dark. Guide your students to see that it's now midnight where you live. Point out that her back is brightest because it is noon on the opposite side of the world.

Day 2

1. Obtain a globe and a beach ball. Label the beach ball "Sun" and have one child stand holding the beach ball in the center of the room. You stand holding the globe. Ask your students these questions: "During which season do we have the most hours of daylight?" (*summer*) "Do you know why?" (*That's when our hemisphere on Earth tilts toward the sun.*)

2. Have the class chorally read the poem "Bed in Summer" on page 50 twice.

3. While the child holding the sun stands still, slowly move around him/her, tilting the globe toward and then away from the sun. Say where it is summer or winter based on the tilting globe.

4. Distribute the graphic organizers. Have the students fill in the "Was I Right?" column. For incorrect statements, students must write an explanation below the statement.

Geography

The Sun's Travels
by Robert Louis Stevenson

The sun is not in bed when I
At night upon my pillow lie.

Still 'round the earth his way he takes,
And morning after morning makes.

While here at home, in shining day,
We 'round the sunny garden play,

Each little Indian sleepyhead
Is being kissed and put in bed.

And when at eve I rise from tea,
Day dawns beyond the Atlantic Sea.

And all the children in the West
Are getting up and being dressed.

Bed in Summer
by Robert Louis Stevenson

In winter I get up at night
And dress by yellow candlelight.

In summer, quite the other way,
I have to go to bed by day.

I have to go to bed and see
The birds still hopping on the tree,

Or hear the grown-up people's feet
Still going past me in the street.

And does it not seem hard to you,
When all the sky is clear and blue,

And I should like so much to play,
To have to go to bed by day?

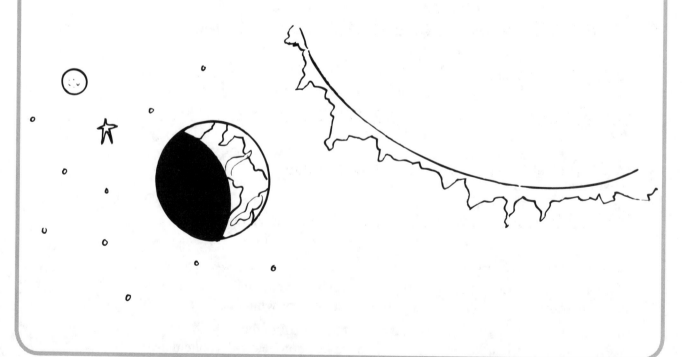

Sample Graphic Organizer

Thinking Guide

Directions: Read each statement. Write an **A** if you agree. Write a **D** if you disagree.
You will fill in the second column later.

Geography

		Me	**Was I Right?**
1. The sun travels around our Earth.		A	N
The Earth travels around the sun.			
2. Earth's tilt causes our seasons to change.		D	N
The Earth moving around the sun and tilting on its axis causes the seasons to change.			
3. As the sun sets on the opposite side of Earth, it rises here.		A	Y
4. The sun is always shining, even at night.		D	N
The sun is always shining. It is just shining on the other side of the world when it is dark here.			
5. We see the sun more hours in the winter than the summer.		D	Y

Directions: Read each statement. Write an **A** if you agree. Write a **D** if you disagree. You will fill in the second column later.

Geography

	Me	Was I Right?

1. _____ _____ _____

_____

_____

2. _____ _____ _____

_____

_____

3. _____ _____ _____

_____

_____

4. _____ _____ _____

_____

_____

5. _____ _____ _____

_____

_____

1. Make a T-chart on the board. Label one column "Continents" and the other "Oceans." Ask your students to name all the continents they can. Then ask them to name all the oceans. Do not correct any misconceptions (for example, if a student says Red Sea for an ocean or Greenland for a continent, write these ideas down).

2. Ask your students to order the continents from largest to smallest, with "1" being the biggest. Do the same with the oceans. Write the numbers of your class's order next to the names in the columns. Do not correct misconceptions.

3. Explain to your class, "We are going to learn about Earth's continents and oceans. We will read about them and fill out a map. Then we will check to see if the information in our chart is accurate."

4. Make and distribute student copies of "Earth's Continents and Oceans" on page 54.

5. Make an overhead transparency and student copies of the "World Map" graphic organizer on page 56.

6. Display the transparency and distribute the student copies of the graphic organizer.

7. Have a volunteer read the first paragraph while the class follows along.

8. Have a volunteer read the second paragraph as the class follows along. Then stop and fill in the continents on the overhead. Ask, "Look at the board. Did we name all of the continents correctly? Did we leave one out? Did we have any extra?" As your students identify errors, add or erase from the "Continents" column of the T-chart.

9. Read aloud the clue about the location of the Atlantic Ocean. Have a student come up and indicate where it is on the transparency. All students should fill it in on their maps.

10. Have a student read aloud the clues about each of the remaining four oceans. Each time have a student come up and indicate where it is on the map. All the students should fill in the oceans on their maps.

11. Ask, "Look at the board. Did we name all of the oceans correctly? Did we leave one out? Did we have any extra?" As your students identify errors, add or erase from the Oceans column of the T-chart.

12. Ask, "Look at the passage. It tells us which oceans are the biggest and smallest. Did we mark them correctly on the board?"

13. Have your students read the clues about the size of the oceans. Use them to lead a class discussion to determine the appropriate order. (*1–Pacific, 2–Atlantic, 3–Indian, 4–Southern, 5–Arctic*) Once you have established the order, mark the numbers on the oceans on the transparency (students should do so at their seats). Then direct the students' attention to the board to check and revise, if necessary, the "Oceans" column of the T-chart.

14. Have a detailed world map available as your students read the clues about the size of the continents in case volunteers need to point out the location of nations mentioned in the clues to their classmates. Use the clues to lead a class discussion to establish the appropriate order. (*1–Asia, 2–Africa, 3–North America, 4–South America, 5–Antarctica, 6–Europe, 7–Australia*). Mark the numbers on the continents on the transparency (students should do so at their seats). Then direct the students' attention to the board to check and revise, if necessary, the "Continents" column of the T-chart.

Geography

Earth's Continents and Oceans

About 200 million years ago, all the land on Earth was joined. It was a supercontinent. One big sea surrounded this landmass. Over a long time, the land broke into huge chunks. The chunks slowly drifted away from each other. They formed seven continents. Five oceans surround them. All the oceans have salty water. They cover 93 percent of Earth's surface.

On one side of Earth lies four continents: Europe, Asia, Africa, and Australia. On the other side lies two continents: North America and South America. At the bottom of Earth lies the continent of Antarctica. Label these continents on your world map.

The Atlantic Ocean lies between North and South America and Europe and Africa. Label it on your map.

The Indian Ocean lies between Africa, Australia, and Asia. Label it on your map.

The Pacific Ocean lies between Asia and the west coasts of North and South America. It is the biggest ocean. Label it on your map.

At Earth's top is its smallest ocean. It lies between the top of North America and the top of Europe and Asia. Ice covers the Arctic Ocean. Label it on your map.

At Earth's bottom is its stormiest sea. It is dangerous to sail there. There are big, wild waves and huge icebergs. This is the ocean that surrounds Antarctica. It is the Southern Ocean. Label it on your map.

Use these clues to figure out the order of size of the five oceans:

1. The world's stormiest sea is the second-smallest ocean.
2. The sea that lies between Australia, Africa, and Asia is the warmest. It is also the third-biggest.

Use these clues to figure out the order of size of the continents:

1. England, France, and Germany lie on the second-smallest continent.
2. China lies on the largest continent.
3. The smallest continent looks like an island off by itself.
4. Mexico lies on the third-biggest continent.
5. Panama joins the fourth-biggest continent to the third biggest. This tiny nation is just 40 miles wide.
6. The world's coldest continent is bigger than Europe but smaller than South America.

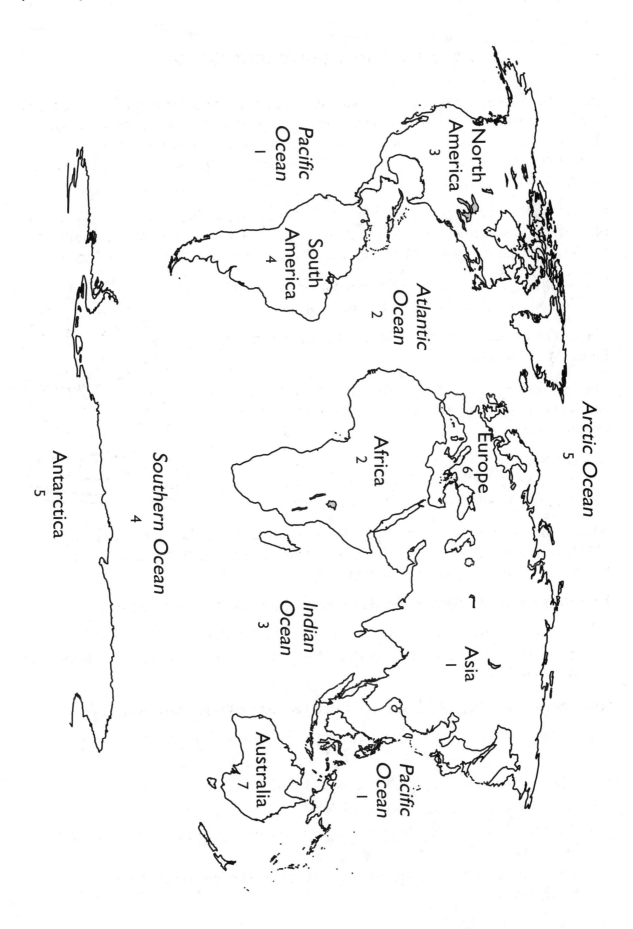

1. This lesson is best taught after the "Earth's Rock Cycle" lesson that begins on page 17. This geography lesson talks about Earth's tectonic plates and erosion, both of which are introduced and discussed in detail in the science lesson. However, if you want to do this lesson separately, be sure that your students understand those concepts first.

2. Write these vocabulary words on the board:

    ✧ **overpass**—a road, pedestrian walkway, railroad, bridge, etc., crossing over another road

    ✧ **Ice Age**—a long period of time during which glaciers covered much of Earth's surface beyond the tropical regions; the last one ended about 10,000 years ago

    ✧ **glaciers**—gigantic ice sheets that slowly flow over a land mass, formed from compacted snow in places where snow accumulates faster than it melts

    ✧ **receded**—pulled back

    ✧ **deposited**—put down; laid down

    ✧ **plateau** (pla-TOH)—a land area having a relatively flat surface much higher than the adjoining land on at least one side and often having a steep side or sides

    ✧ **prairie** (PRAIR-ee)—a flat tract of grassland; a plain

    Ask the students to volunteer the definitions for these terms. Provide the definitions for any they do not know.

3. Make and distribute student copies of "Earth's Landforms" on page 58. It is written at a 3.5 reading level, so depending upon the needs of your class, you can have the students read it as a whole group, in pairs, or independently.

4. Discuss the article.

5. Make an overhead transparency and student copies of the "Classification Chart" graphic organizer on page 60.

6. Display the transparency and distribute the student copies.

7. Explain that this chart is a way to make notes about the landforms article. Since it is a "skeleton" format, most of the information will be brief and not in complete sentences.

8. For the box at the top, ask students to generate the main idea. Guide them to generate the one shown on the completed graphic organizer on page 59. Write it in the box while they do so at their seats.

9. Explain that the information in the graphic organizer will range from general to more specific as you move down the levels.

10. Tell your students that often in textbooks or articles, key terms are put in italics or boldface print. This makes the term stand out so that as you reread to take notes or study, you can quickly scan the page for the different-looking text. In this piece, the key terms are in italics. Have your students use highlighters to mark these words. They will go into the boxes below the main idea. (Help your students to understand that "plain" will go in the box and information about flood plains and prairies will go beneath it (since both are kinds of plains).)

11. One paragraph at a time, guide your class to identify the three major points about each type of landform and then write them in the appropriate location on the classification chart.

12. When you come to the last paragraph, explain that the information in it relates to mountains, hills, and plateaus and add the landslide statement to those sections.

Earth's Landforms

Our Earth has many different landforms. There are hills and valleys. There are mountains and plains. How did they form? Why are they where they are?

We created some landforms. We used power equipment to dig out some areas and build up others. A highway overpass shows an example of a landform that we made. We wanted one road to go over another. So we used bulldozers to make small hills on both sides of the lower road. Then we built a bridge to join these hills.

Most landforms were created by nature. A *mountain* rises as least 1,000 feet above the land around it. Volcanoes formed some mountains. Other mountains formed when two of Earth's large plates pushed against each other. One plate slid down. The other plate pushed up. The Himalayan Mountains formed this way. They are the tallest mountains on Earth.

Hills are not as tall as mountains, but they are much higher than the surrounding area. Most hills formed from glaciers. During the Ice Age, glaciers covered much of Earth's surface. When the planet grew warmer, these ice sheets melted. As they shrunk, or receded, they dragged bits of rock and soil with them. The rocks and dirt were scraped from some places and deposited in others. When a lot was dropped in one area, it formed a hill.

Erosion wears away at mountains and hills. Wind, water, and ice slowly wear away the rocks on the mountain. Erosion is what forms *valleys*. A valley is the low-lying land between mountains or hills. Often, water formed the valley. Water started in the high area and flowed downhill. Over a long time, it wore away a deep groove called a valley. Valleys with steep sides are called gorges or canyons.

A *flood plain* is the flat area around the river flowing through a valley. A flood plain forms from the mud and dirt left when the river overflows its banks. The river carried these materials away from the land upstream. The floods usually occur each year. A flood plain can be a great area for growing crops, as in the Nile River Valley. Plains, or prairies, are large areas of flat land. They are planted with crops, too.

A *plateau* is a hill or a mountain with a flat top. A plateau may have steep sides called cliffs. A plateau may have started out as a plain. Erosion removed all but the hard rock. So, the hard rock remains on top of the plateau, while its sides wore away.

Earthquakes can change landforms. They can push some land higher and make other land drop lower. This forms ridges. But most often earthquakes cause landslides that change the shape of mountains, hills, or plateaus.

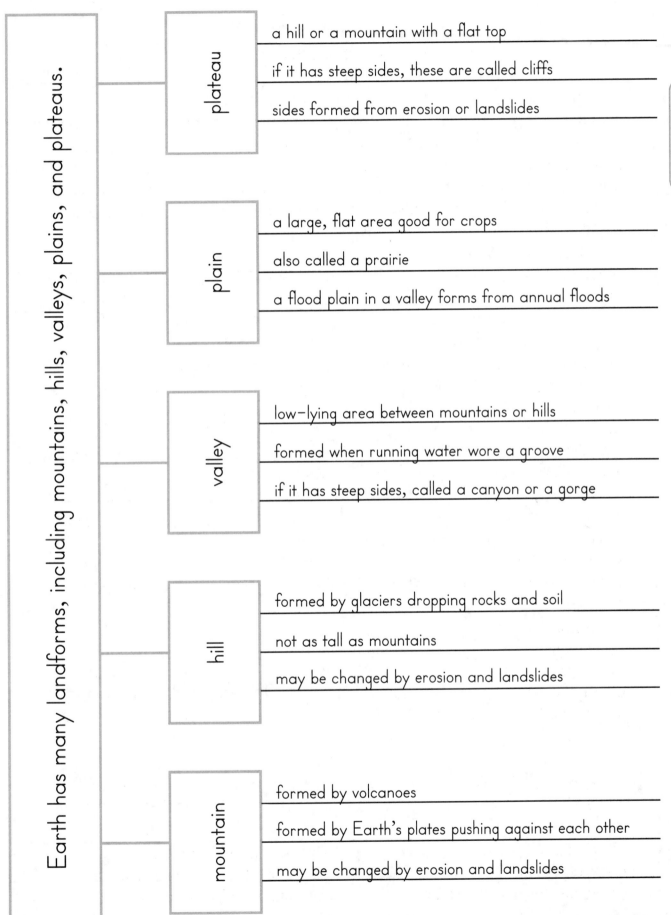

Earth has many landforms, including mountains, hills, valleys, plains, and plateaus.

plateau
- a hill or a mountain with a flat top
- if it has steep sides, these are called cliffs
- sides formed from erosion or landslides

plain
- a large, flat area good for crops
- also called a prairie
- a flood plain in a valley forms from annual floods

valley
- low-lying area between mountains or hills
- formed when running water wore a groove
- if it has steep sides, called a canyon or a gorge

hill
- formed by glaciers dropping rocks and soil
- not as tall as mountains
- may be changed by erosion and landslides

mountain
- formed by volcanoes
- formed by Earth's plates pushing against each other
- may be changed by erosion and landslides

Geography

Day 1

1. Bring in a set of dominoes. Set them up so that when you knock down the first one, it hits the second, which hits the third, etc., to form a chain reaction in which all the dominoes fall down. Ask students to predict what will happen if you knock down the first one.

2. Invite a student to come up and gently knock over the first domino. Have the class watch the chain reaction. Call it a chain reaction. Explain that environmental events can cause chain reactions, too. Give this example of acid rain:

   Factory smokestacks belch smoke into the air. The smoke is filled with sulfur dioxide and nitrogen oxide. Winds carry these chemicals far away to the Adirondack Mountains, where there are no factories. Then it rains or snows. The raindrops or snowflakes contain sulfuric acid. Over years, this makes the lakes have too much acid. Fish and other wildlife die. The pine trees surrounding the lakes can die, too.

3. Make student copies of "Ecosystems: Balance Is a Must" on page 62. Introduce any unfamiliar vocabulary:

   ❖ **community**—all of the organisms (plants, animals, and microscopic life) that live in a particular area

   ❖ **interact**—to act together or with one another

   ❖ **consumer**—an organism, usually an animal, that eats something. There are a few plants that do so, as well (or example, the Venus flytrap is a plant that is a consumer of insects).

   ❖ **West Nile virus**—a disease spread by mosquito bites that occurs in Africa, Asia, the Mediterranean, and parts of North America

   ❖ **predators**—animals that eat meat (other animals)

   ❖ **prey**—animals that are eaten by other animals

   ❖ **stabilized**—made steady; kept from fluctuation

4. Distribute the student copies. This article is written at a 3.6 reading level, so you may wish to have your students read it as a whole class, in partner groups, or independently.

5. Discuss the article.

Day 2

1. Make an overhead transparency and student copies of the "Chain Reaction" graphic organizer on page 64.

2. Display the transparency and distribute the student copies.

3. As a whole class, fill in the graphic organizer based on the Isle Royale ecosystem imbalance. You are doing this one as a whole group because it is the more challenging scenario.

Day 3

1. Make new student copies of the "Chain Reaction" graphic organizer.

2. Pair the students. Have them reread the West Nile virus ecosystem imbalance scenario and use the information about it to fill in their graphic organizers. Here's what they should write on the eight dominoes: *West Nile virus killed crows. The dead crows fell to the ground and rotted. Bacteria fed on their dead bodies and reproduced. Soon there was too much bacteria. This killed the plants. Mice who ate the plants left or died. The skunks and snakes that ate the mice left or died. The owls and hawks that ate the snakes and skunks left or died.*

3. Collect these graphic organizers to check for understanding.

Geography

Ecosystems: Balance Is a Must

An ecosystem is a community of plants and animals. They live in the same area. They interact with each other. They interact with their environment. Ecosystems are based on food webs. This means that an ecosystem must stay in balance. If it gets out of balance, food webs fall apart. Plants and animals start to die. Why? If there are too many plant eaters, they will ruin the plant population. They will eat the plants faster than the plants can grow back. And if there are too many animal consumers, they will run out of food.

How do scientists know that this is true? They have watched it happen. Not long ago, the West Nile virus killed a lot of crows. The birds fell to the ground. Their bodies rotted. Bacteria in the dirt fed on the dead birds. The bacteria multiplied. Soon the number of bacteria grew too large. Plants died from too many bacteria in the soil. Then mice could not find enough food. They starved or left the area. This meant that the snakes and skunks that ate the mice did not have enough food. They starved or left, too. The hawks and owls that ate the snakes and skunks ran out of food, too. So a sickness that killed one just kind of organism caused a chain reaction. It wrecked the whole community.

Fortunately, ecosystems can recover. But it takes many years. What happened on Isle Royale is a good example. In the 1920s a pair of moose left the Canadian shore. They swam out to Isle Royale in Lake Superior. They were the only large animals there. There were no predators to eat them. By 1930, there were 3,000 moose! The moose ate the plants faster than the plants could grow back. In 1933, the moose began to starve. Their numbers dropped. With fewer moose, the plants grew back. Over time, the moose population grew again.

In 1950 a pair of wolves swam out to the island. They ate the moose. The number of wolves grew. Then there got to be too many wolves. They did not have enough prey. They started to starve. After many years, the ecosystem stabilized on Isle Royale. There were 600 moose and 20 wolves. There were just enough moose and just enough wolves to keep them both from starving. It had taken decades, but at last the ecosystem was in balance.

Sample Graphic Organizer

Chain Reaction

Geography

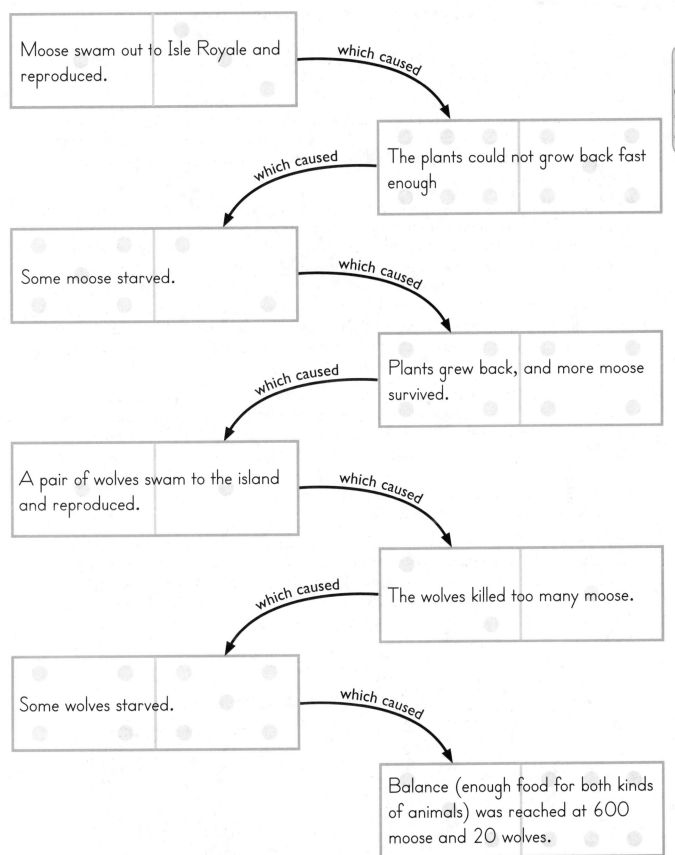

©*Teacher Created Resources, Inc.*   63   *#8093 Content Area Lessons Using Graphic Organizers*

Geography

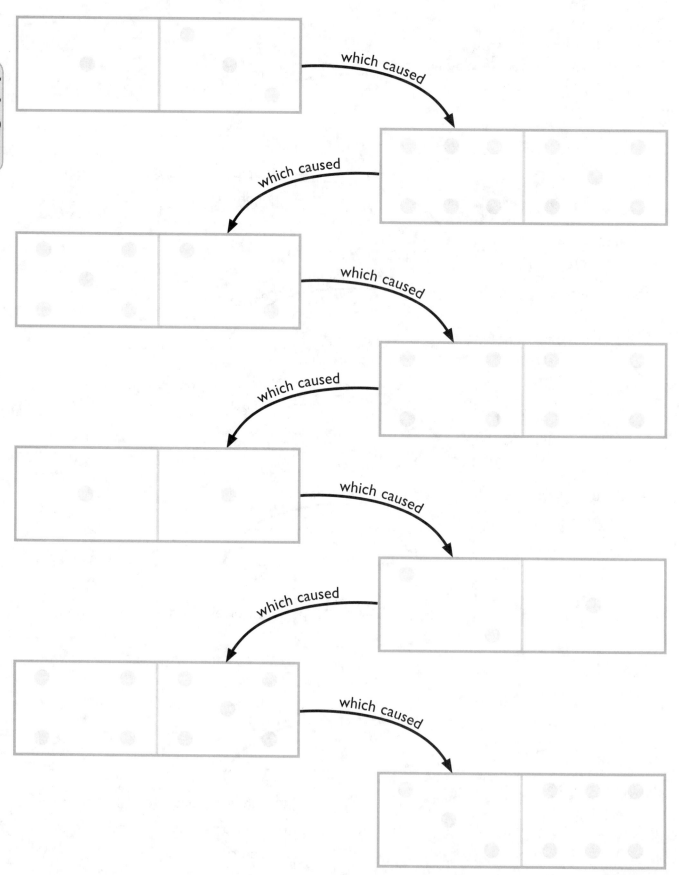

1. Introduce any unfamiliar vocabulary:

   ✧ **transfers**—moves

   ✧ **wry**—lopsided

   ✧ **tool-house**—shed

   ✧ **till**—abbreviation of "until" to make it one syllable

   ✧ **horrorful**—a word invented by the author to mean full of horror; explain that sometimes poets invent words because, as in this case, they need them for a rhyme.

2. Discuss the importance of "making a movie in your mind" as you read. Making mental images in your mind is one of the best ways to enjoy and understand text, as well as remember what you've read. Ask your students to close their eyes and keep them closed during this guided visualization exercise.

3. Make student copies of the poem "Mr. Macklin's Jack O' Lantern" on page 66 but don't distribute them yet. Read the poem aloud to your class.

4. Have the students open their eyes and discuss what they visualized. Ask your class, "Did you make a movie in your mind of the events happening in Mr. Macklin's tool-house? Which image was the most memorable? Do you think this 'movie' will help you to remember this poem?"

5. Pass out copies of the poem and read it again as the students follow along. Then, re-read it chorally. Discuss why the author put the last line in italics. (*for emphasis*)

6. Write this question on the board: "Picture in your mind what happened inside Mr. Macklin's tool-house. What are the five main events?" Have your students read the poem again silently to answer this question.

7. Discuss the five main events. (*Mr. Macklin carves Jack's face; Mr. Macklin puts his pipe in Jack's mouth; everyone laughs; Mr. Macklin draws the shade; Mr. Macklin lights a candle inside Jack and it causes scary shadows.*)

8. Make an overhead transparency and student copies of the "Movie Film" graphic organizer on page 68.

9. Display the transparency. Explain that this is what movie films look like. Movie film comes on a big reel and is shown with a projector in theaters.

10. Ask a student to read the first stanza. Draw a picture of Mr. Macklin's jack o' lantern in the first film frame. Ask the students to give you details from the poem to make the picture accurate (*has two eyes, a nose, and seven teeth in the mouth*).

11. Distribute the student copies of the graphic organizer. Have your students draw the next four events (see above) in the remaining sections of the film. They should show details and colors in their pictures. Discuss things that must be included based on information given (*such as Jack should have seven teeth in each picture; the corncob pipe should be yellow/tan color*) and things that can be added from imagination (*such as what Mr. Macklin looks like and how many children are there*).

12. Collect their completed graphic organizers and check for understanding.

Mr. Macklin's Jack O' Lantern
by David McCord

Mr. Macklin takes his knife
And carves the yellow pumpkin face:
Three holes bring eyes and nose to life;
The mouth has seven teeth in place.

Then Mr. Macklin, just for fun,
Transfers the corn cob pipe from his
Wry mouth to Jack's, and everyone
Dies laughing! O what fun it is!

Till Mr. Macklin draws the shade
And lights the candle in Jack's skull
Then all the inside dark is made
As spooky and as horrorful

As Halloween, and creepy crawl
The shadows on the tool-house floor.
With Jack's face dancing on the wall.
Oh, Mr. Macklin! Where's the door?

Reading

Day 1

1. Make student copies of "The Tiger and the Wild Bull" on page 70. Introduce any unfamiliar vocabulary:

    ✧ **bull**—a male cattle
    ✧ **gore**—stab
    ✧ **brambles**—thorny bushes
    ✧ **splintered**—shattered

2. Explain that most societies had folktales to teach listeners lessons about how to live. This folktale originated in the nation of India. (Show your students where it is on a map).

3. Ask these questions prior to reading the folktale:

    • What animals can you assume lived there in the past? (*Tigers and cattle must be native to India for the people to have used them as characters in their stories.*)
    • In this story, the tiger is a villain. Why do you think the Indians had a tiger be the villain? (*Tigers attack people, too, so they weren't well-liked!*)
    • What do you know about tigers?
    • What do you know about cattle?

4. Have your students read the folktale. It is written at a 2.2 reading level.

Day 2

1. Read the folktale again. Since this is a second reading, you can make it more challenging—for example, having the students read it independently instead of in pairs. If the students read aloud, they should do so with greater fluency because they already know the text.

2. Make an overhead transparency and student copies of the "Somebody-Wanted-But-So" graphic organizer on page 72. This graphic organizer will help your students to understand cause-and-effect relationships.

3. Display the transparency and distribute the student copies. Fill in the transparency while the students do so at their seats. Start out by writing the tiger in the "Somebody" column. Ask your students to tell what the tiger wanted (*to kill the bull*) and write that in the "Wanted" column.

4. Explain that the word *but* means that something was preventing the tiger from getting what she wanted. Then ask, "What should we write in the 'But' column?" (*The bull had dangerous horns.*)

5. The word *so* indicates that something happens because of the info in the "But" column. Ask, "What did the tiger do because the bull had dangerous horns? That's what we'll write in the 'So' column." (*She told the bull he would be much more handsome without the horns.*)

6. Now read the first row of the graphic organizer: "The tiger wanted to kill the bull, but the bull had dangerous horns. So the tiger told the bull he would be much more handsome without the horns."

7. Pair the students. Ask them to fill in the second row of the graphic organizer. Give them about five minutes.

8. Reconvene and go over what should be written in the second row.

9. Explain that folktales were meant to teach morals in an interesting, memorable way. Ask them what they learned from this story. Discuss until you reach an agreement on the moral and write it at the bottom of the graphic organizer.

Reading

The Tiger and the Wild Bull

One day a tiger sat in some bushes watching a fat bull as he grazed in a field. She wanted to bring home some meat to her cubs.

"If only he didn't have those sharp horns," thought the tiger. "Then I could easily make a feast of him. As it is, he might gore me. I could end up dead."

Then she had a clever idea. Quietly slipping up beside the bull, the tiger said in a friendly tone, "What a handsome beast you are! I've been admiring you from the bushes. You have such big, powerful shoulders and strong legs. I am curious, though. Why do you keep those horns on your head? Carrying them around must give you a headache, and they ruin your otherwise perfect appearance."

"Do you really think so?" asked the bull. "Why, I never thought about it. But now that you mention it, these horns often do get in my way. Just last week I got tangled up in some brambles because of them. I was trapped for an hour. And they ruin my appearance? Hmmm. . . ."

The tiger went away. She hid behind a tree to see what the bull would do. The bull waited until the tiger was gone. The he started hitting his horns against a rock with all his might. His right horn splintered. Then he smashed his left horn. At last the bull stood up proudly with his head smooth and bare.

"Now I've got you!" snarled the tiger as she jumped from her hiding place. "Thanks for getting rid of your horns. They were what kept you from becoming my cubs' next meal."

Title: The Tiger and the Wild Bull

Somebody	Wanted	But	So
the tiger	to kill the wild bull so that her cubs would have meat to eat	the bull had dangerous horns	the tiger told the bull that he would look much better without horns
the bull	to be more handsome	he thought he had to destroy his horns	the tiger was able to kill the bull once the bull got rid of his horns

What can we learn from this story?

Someone may say nice things to you because they want to trick you

or get something from you.

Reading

Title: _____

Somebody	Wanted	But	So

What can we learn from this story?

_____

_____

Day 1

1. This lesson is designed to show your students how to use a dictionary. If possible, pass out a dictionary to each one of them and demonstrate how to look up these words: *eel, uncommonly,* and *somersault*. Note that many of your students may know the meaning of the word *somersault* but not immediately recognize the word in print.

2. It's important to directly show your students how to use the guide words, how to figure out the pronunciation given in parentheses, which syllable is accented, and the part of speech (often given in italics). Nouns and adverbs are the parts of speech covered in this lesson.

3. See if your students can define a noun (*a word that is a person, place, or thing*). Give them the definition of an adverb (*a word that describes/modifies a verb (an action word) or an adjective (a describing word)*). Give them some examples of nouns and adverbs; many words ending with the letters *ly* are adverbs: *slowly, accidentally, quickly,* etc.

4. Make and distribute student copies of the poem "You Are Old, Father William" on page 74.

5. Read the poem chorally as a whole class. Then have the students take turns reading each stanza based on gender (boys read first stanza, girls read the second, and so forth) or halves of the room.

6. Discuss the poem's meter (each stanza has 11 beats in the first and third lines and 9 beats in the second and fourth lines) and how it is based on the number of syllables in each line.

7. Make an overhead transparency and student copies of the "Dictionary Definitions" graphic organizer on page 76.

8. Display the transparency and distribute the student copies and a dictionary (if possible) to each student. If that's not possible, have groups share a dictionary and each classmate take a turn looking up a word.

9. As a class, look up the first four words in bold print in the poem: *incessantly, sage, locks, ointment*. The guide words given at the top of the dictionary page must be written on the graphic organizer, as well as the word you looked up, its pronunciation (have them underline the accented syllable), part of speech, and definition. Help your students to decide which definition to write for *locks and sage* based on its context in the poem.

Day 2

1. Reread the poem chorally to develop fluency.

2. As a class, look up the remaining four words in bold print: *shilling, pound, suet, airs*. When the class looks up the definition for *shilling*, they will have problems understanding that it's part of a pound—in fact, they may think it's a measure of weight. So explain that sometimes when you look up a word, it will have a word in the definition that you don't understand, and so you'll have to look up that word (in this case, *pound*). Also, help your students to decide on the definition for *airs* based on its context in the poem.

3. Be sure to discuss the hyperbole (gross exaggeration) used in the poem. Ask your students to give examples of hyperbole: no one incessantly stands on his head; Father William says he's sure he has no brain; no one actually eats the bones and beak of a goose; nobody can balance an eel on the end of his or her nose.

You Are Old, Father William

by Lewis Carroll

"You are old, Father William," the young man said.
"And your hair has become very white;
and yet you **incessantly** stand on your head.
Do you think, at your age, it is right?"

"In my youth," Father William replied to his son,
"I feared it might injure the brain.
But now that I'm perfectly sure I have none,
why, I do it again and again."

"You are old," said the youth. "As I mentioned before,
and have grown most uncommonly fat;
Yet you turned a back somersault in at the door.
Pray, what was the reason for that?"

"In my youth," said the **sage**, as he shook his gray **locks**.
"I kept all my limbs very supple
by use of this **ointment**—one **shilling** a box.
Allow me to sell you a couple?"

"You are old," said the youth. "And your jaws are too weak
for anything tougher than **suet**.
Yet you finished the goose with the bones and the beak.
Pray, how did you manage to do it?"

"In my youth," said his father. "I took to the law,
and argued each case with my wife.
And the muscular strength which it gave to my jaw
has lasted the rest of my life."

"You are old," said the youth. "One would hardly suppose
that your eye was as steady as ever;
Yet you balanced an eel on the end of your nose.
What made you so awfully clever?"

"I have answered three questions and that is enough," said his father.
"Don't give yourself **airs!**
Do you think I can listen all day to such stuff?
Be off, or I'll kick you downstairs!"

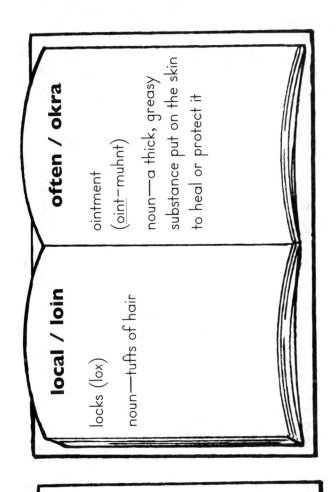

often / okra

ointment
(oint–muhnt)

noun—a thick, greasy
substance put on the skin
to heal or protect it

local / loin

locks (lox)

noun—tufts of hair

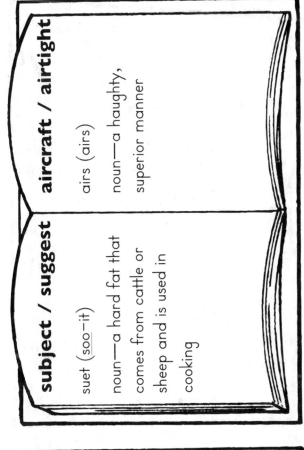

aircraft / airtight

airs (airs)

noun—a haughty,
superior manner

subject / suggest

suet (soo–it)

noun—a hard fat that
comes from cattle or
sheep and is used in
cooking

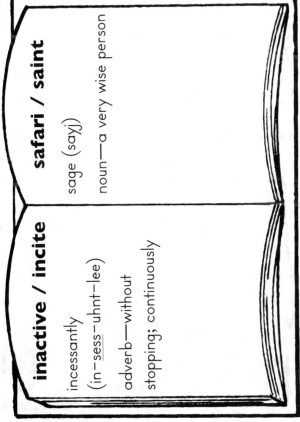

safari / saint

sage (sayj)

noun—a very wise person

inactive / incite

incessantly
(in–sess–uhnt–lee)

adverb—without
stopping; continuously

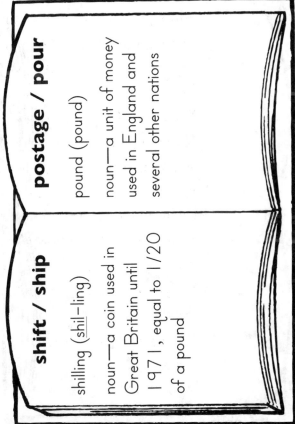

postage / pour

pound (pound)

noun—a unit of money
used in England and
several other nations

shift / ship

shilling (shil–ling)

noun—a coin used in
Great Britain until
1971, equal to 1/20
of a pound

Reading

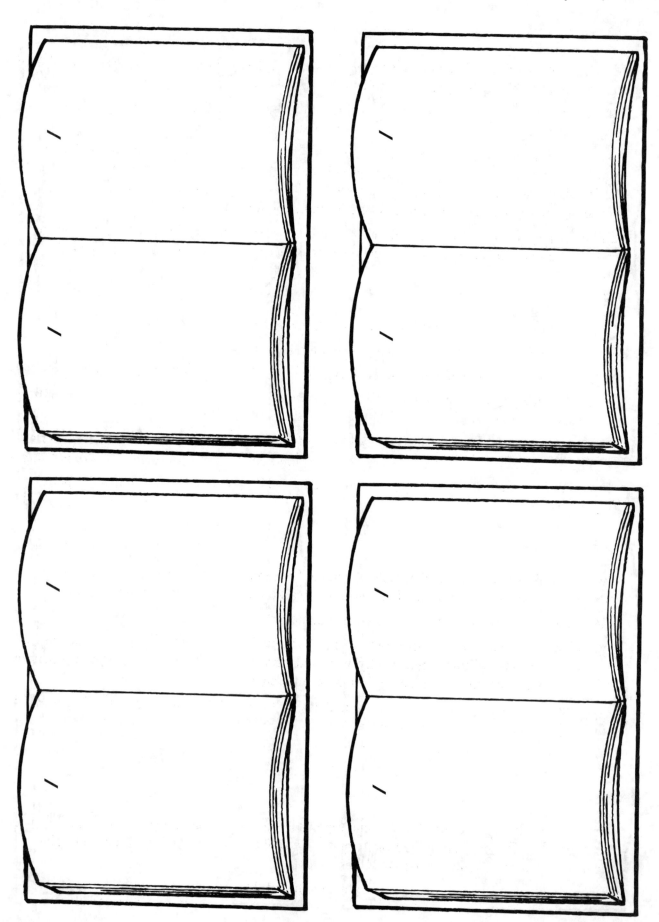

Day 1

1. Gather simple nonfiction books on a variety of animals. The books should have at least a table of contents or an index or they are too simplistic for this lesson.

2. For this project, your students will not be using online resources. They are learning to use a book's index, table of contents, etc., to locate information.

3. Pose a question, such as, "Where do flamingoes live?" Then choose an appropriate book and show your students how to use the index or table of contents to look up information about flamingoes. Draw the analogy that an index is like a search engine on the Internet. You need to choose the appropriate search terms in order to find the information you seek.

4. Turn to the page about flamingoes. Read it aloud to your students. Did it answer your question? If not, try another resource. Show students that persistence is required when doing research.

Day 2

1. Make and display an overhead transparency of "Use a Book Wisely" on page 78.

2. Ask questions for the students to answer by reading the transparency:

   • Look at the table of contents. On what page does the chapter about odd mammals begin? (*23*)

   • Look at the glossary. What does the word *primates* mean? (*the group of mammals that has hands instead of paws*)

   • Look at the index. On what pages would you find information about gorillas? (*56, 113–115*)

   • Look at the index. Does this book have information on antelopes? (*no, not listed in the index*)

   • Look at the index entry for cats. On what pages would you find information about pets? (*50–51*)

Days 3–4

1. Make an overhead copy of the completed "Animal Research Outline" graphic organizer on page 79 and student copies of the blank "Animal Research Outline" organizer on page 80.

2. Display the overhead and distribute the student copies.

3. Point out how the student who filled out the transparency did not write in complete sentences because she was taking notes. She briefly answered each question. She will turn the information into sentences and paragraphs as she writes the actual report.

4. Have your students select an animal in which they are interested in doing research. They will fill in the graphic organizer about this animal.

5. Allow them ample time to do the research.

Day 5

1. Students write their first draft of the animal report. Let them use the same sequence as the research outline in formulating their paragraphs. Be sure to circulate as they compose to give guidance and to prompt those who get writer's block.

2. Have the students make a drawing or cut out a picture of their animal and put it on a separate sheet of paper.

Reading

Use a Book Wisely

A table of contents appears at the start of a nonfiction book. It lists the chapter titles in order.

A glossary appears near the back of a nonfiction book. It gives the definitions for terms used in the book. It's like a very short dictionary.

Glossary

carnivore—an animal that eats only meat (other animals)

fertilize—to provide what is needed for new life to start

habitat—the place where animals live in nature

herbivore—an animal that eats only plants

omnivore—an animal that eats both plants and animals

prey—an animal that is hunted and eaten by other animals

primates—the group of mammals that has hands (often with thumbs) instead of paws

vertebrate—an animal that has a spine (backbone)

An index appears on the last page(s) of a nonfiction book. It lists the topics and important words in the book in alphabetical order and on which page(s) they appear.

1. What is its name?

snapping turtle; snapper

2. What kind of animal (mammal, reptile, insect, etc.) is it?

reptile with a shell

3. Where does it live?

common snapper = North America, Central America, and parts of South America in ponds and swamps

alligator snapper = central and southeastern U.S. swamps

4. How long does it live?

up to 70 years (maybe as long as 100)

5. What does it look like?

shell with rough edges, sharp pointed beak, strong jaws, tiny black eyes

can grow to be 19 to 36 inches long; alligator can weigh 200 pounds

6. What does it eat?

small fish, frogs, snakes, other turtles, insects, snails, baby geese and ducklings and some plants

7. How does it reproduce?

first mate when 12 years old

female lays around 36 eggs in a hole in the ground in spring

babies hatch in early fall (become boys if dirt is warm; girls if dirt is cool)

8. Who or what are its enemies?

humans (especially for the alligator snapper)

9. Is it endangered? If yes, why?

yes, because people like to eat it

10. Is this animal important to people? If yes, in what way?

The alligator snapper is eaten as soup in Louisiana.

Reading

I. What is its name?

2. What kind of animal (mammal, reptile, insect, etc.) is it?

3. Where does it live?

4. How long does it live?

5. What does it look like?

6. What does it eat?

7. How does it reproduce?

8. Who or what are its enemies?

9. Is it endangered? If yes, why?

10. Is this animal important to people? If yes, in what way?

Day 1

1. This lesson is meant to immediately follow the lesson on nonfiction-book features that begins on page 77. However, this lesson can be done independently after your students have written any type of expository report and need to get feedback on the first draft.

2. One of the most important steps of the writing process is editing. Peer editing is one way for students to get help in practicing this valuable skill. Make a poster of the steps and post it in a prominent location in your classroom:

   - **Praise:** "What did you like best about the report?"

   - **Question:** "What questions do you have?"

   - **Polish:** "What thing(s) could be added?" "What thing(s) could be removed?

   Go over the poster and explain the process of peer review and editing.

3. Make and distribute student copies of the "Snapping Turtle" report on page 82.

4. Make and display an overhead transparency of the blank "Praise-Question-Polish" graphic organizer on page 84.

5. Read the "Snapping Turtle" report aloud to the class. Then have them reread it silently.

6. Fill in the graphic organizer at the overhead as the students give you ideas. If they give you overtly wrong ideas—such as the report is poorly organized—gently guide them to understand that it is not poorly organized. Remind them that they aren't trying to find things to complain about; they are simply commenting on what's great about the report and what, in their opinion, can be improved. It is not their role to correct spelling or grammatical errors.

7. The completed graphic organizer on page 83 is just for your information; you should use the students' own comments.

Day 2

1. Make and distribute student copies of the "Praise-Question-Polish" graphic organizer on page 84.

2. After students have written a first draft of their animal report, they meet with a partner. The first student reads aloud his or her paper. Then the student listens to the other student read aloud his or her report.

3. Next, the students exchange papers and read each other's work silently. They are not to write or make marks of any kind on each other's papers.

4. Have the students independently complete the graphic organizer and submit it to you. Check the graphic organizers for understanding.

Day 3

1. Return the graphic organizers back to the animal-report authors. Explain that the authors have the option of using or ignoring their editors' advice. They can confer with their editors if necessary.

2. The students prepare the final draft of the animal report and submit it to you.

Writing

Snapping Turtles

Snapping turtles are scary reptiles. They are called snappers. They live in fresh water in North America, Central America, and parts of South America. There are two kinds. One is the common snapper. It lives in ponds from Canada to Ecuador. It grows to be 19 inches long.

The other kind is the alligator snapper. It lives in swamps in the central and southeastern United States. An alligator snapper is the biggest freshwater turtle in North America. It can grow more than three feet long. It can weigh more than 200 pounds!

All snapping turtles have shells with rough edges. They have big heads with black eyes and a sharp beak. Snappers have strong jaws. They can crush bones in one bite. A snapper cannot pull its head and legs inside its shell. So it relies on its bite for defense. And it can reach its head around almost to its back legs if something grabs it from behind.

Snapping turtles eat small fish, frogs, snakes, other turtles, insects, snails, and baby geese and ducklings. They eat underwater plants, too.

Snappers have to reach 12 years old. Then they can reproduce. They mate in spring. The female leaves the water. She digs a hole. She lays about 36 eggs. Then she covers the nest and goes away. The sex of the baby turtles is based on the dirt's temperature. If the dirt is warm, the babies are males. If the dirt is cool, they are females. The eggs hatch in the early fall.

Snappers can live a long time. Some have lived 70 years. Scientists think they may be able to live 100 years. Humans are their main predator. Alligator snapping turtles are endangered. People in Louisiana catch them. They eat them in soup.

Trisha Bennett   Ahamed Alkaeer
_____   _____
writer's name   **editor's name**

PRAISE

The part I like the best __is how strong a snapping turtle's jaws are.__

_____

_____

QUESTION

I do not understand __how snapping turtles grow up after they hatch.__

_____

_____

POLISH

Maybe you should add __which animals eat snapping turtles.__

_____

_____

Maybe you should get rid of __the list of all the animals snapping turtles will eat.__

__Just tell the most common ones.__

_____

Writing

_____   _____
writer's name   **editor's name**

PRAISE

The part I like the best _____

_____

_____

QUESTION

I do not understand _____

_____

_____

POLISH

Maybe you should add _____

_____

_____

Maybe you should get rid of _____

_____

_____

Day 1

1. Introduce the concept of prefixes (additions to the beginning of words that change their meanings). Give a few examples. Write the base word, ask what it means, then add the prefix (without the hyphen): *out-grown, out-doors, pre-pay,* and *pre-heat.* Help students figure out what these two prefixes mean *(out* means "beyond" and *pre* means "before").

2. Explain that they are going to study the prefix *re-,* which means "again."

3. Write these words on the board and ask your students to tell you the opposite of each:

   - wet (dry)
   - cold (hot)
   - dark (light)
   - tall (short)
   - inside (outside)

4. Explain that they are going to study the prefix *dis-,* which means "opposite of."

5. Make and display an overhead transparency of the "Cap the Pen" graphic organizer on page 88.

6. One at a time, write the examples given on the completed graphic organizer on page 87. Show the students how to put the word parts together to form a word and write it on the line. Discuss the meaning of each word and how you know that meaning from its parts.

7. Ask for student volunteers to generate sentences for each of the words. Write them on the board or on chart paper.

8. Keep the graphic organizer displayed on the screen. Have the students choose two of the words from it and write a sentence for each. Collect these papers to check for understanding.

Day 2

1. Write these words in parts on the "Cap the Pen" graphic organizer on page 88: *re-paint, re-appear, dis-belief, dis-trust, dis-like.* Then make copies and distribute them to the students.

2. Have the students join the cap to the pen to form the complete words and write them in the place provided. The students then write the meaning of each based on the word parts (no dictionary use).

3. Have the students write a sentence for each of the words on the back of the paper. Collect and check for understanding.

4. Make student copies of "Working with Words" on page 86. Do the first two with the class. (*1. resubmit; 2. disagrees*) Have the students complete the page for homework.

Day 3

1. Have students exchange papers and correct the homework. (*3. reheating; 4. displeased; 5. disappeared; 6. reenter*)

2. Discuss the meaning of each of the words on the "Cap the Pen" graphic organizer the students completed yesterday. Read aloud a few of the best sentences generated by the students.

Note: The "Cap the Pen" graphic organizer can be used with math problems. You can put numbers on the cap and pen and add subtraction, addition, multiplication, or division symbols between the cap and the pen.

Writing

The prefix *re*- means "again."

The prefix *dis*- means "opposite of."

reenter	resubmit	reheating
disappeared	displeased	disagrees

Directions: Choose a word from the box to complete the sentence. Each word is used once.

1. The teacher told us to fix our mistakes and then _____ our test papers.

   _____ means _____

2. If anyone _____ with this plan, please say so now.

   _____ means _____

3. Their father was _____ the leftovers from Tuesday's dinner.

   _____ means _____

4. From the look on Scott's face, Kara could tell he was _____.

   _____ means _____

5. Although we looked all over, the cat seemed to have just _____.

   _____ means _____

6. A sign stated, "If you leave, you cannot _____ the fairgrounds."

   _____ means _____

Writing

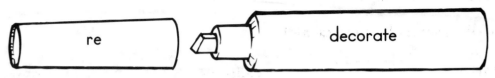

"redecorate" means "to decorate again"

I want to redecorate my bedroom.

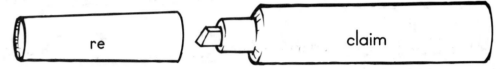

"reclaim" means "to claim again"

We went to reclaim our bag.

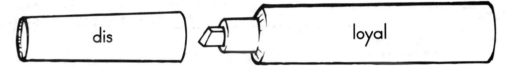

"disloyal" means "the opposite of loyal"

He was so disloyal that he told everyone my secret.

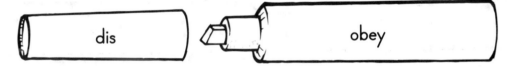

"disobey" means "the opposite of obey"

It is dangerous to disobey safety rules.

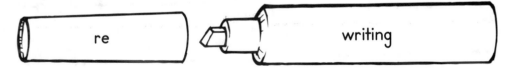

"rewriting" means "writing again"

I am rewriting my report to make it better.

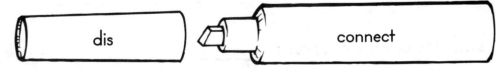

"disconnect" means "the opposite of connect"

Don't disconnect the cord for my keyboard.

Writing

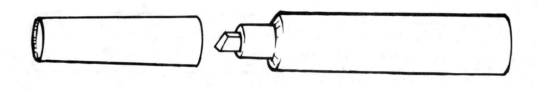

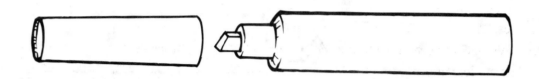

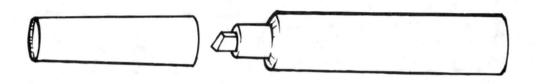

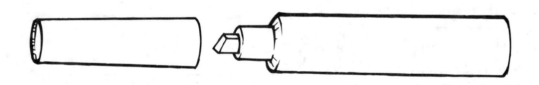

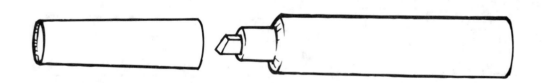

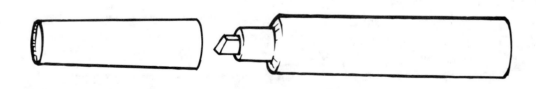

Day 1

1. Explain that a person writes about his or her own life in an autobiography.
2. Make an overhead transparency and student copies of the "Zig Zag Time Line" organizer on page 92. Make a transparency of the parent letter, fill in the ages for yourself, and cut out the pictures. Select at least two pictures about which you recall interesting anecdotes.
3. Display the transparency of the time line. Tell the children that you are creating a time line of events from your life. You'll use this time line to write your autobiography.
4. Show your students the pictures you cut from the transparency. Pick the two for which you have anecdotes. Ask your students to choose five more.
5. Ask individuals to come up and put the pictures in chronological order on the time line.
6. Show the students how to use the data to write a brief autobiography. Start with your birthdate. Then, as the students dictate the information to you, compose on the board. For example:

   I was born on May 1, 1972. I could feed myself with a spoon at the age of one. By 2½, I knew how to dress myself. At the age of three, I went to preschool. When I was four, I learned to ride a bike with training wheels. I was about 5½ when I first tied my shoes and pumped a swing. I lost my first tooth when I was six.

7. Read aloud your autobiography. Note that it is dull. Tell them that by adding anecdotes, it will be more interesting. Prepare and distribute an improved version. For example:

   I was born on May 1, 1972. I could feed myself with a spoon at the age of one. But that doesn't mean I was neat! There's a photo of me with more spaghetti on my face than my plate. By 2 ½, I knew how to dress myself. At the age of three, I went to preschool. My teacher's name was Mrs. Wallace, but I called her "Mrs. Walrus." My last name was Berry, so I thought that everyone had a last name that was a real word.

   When I was four, I learned to ride a bike with training wheels. I had a hard time learning how to balance. I wouldn't let my dad take off my training wheels for two years! I lost my first tooth when I was six. I cried because I tasted the blood from my gums. Yuck! And it happened on the day I had my school photo taken. So there's a big gap between my teeth in the picture.

8. Have the class chorally read your revised autobiography.
9. Make student copies of the parent letter on page 90. Ask the children to have their parents to fill in the paper and return it the next day.

Day 2

1. Have the children cut out the pictures from the parent letter and arrange them in order. (If a parent did not complete the paper, have the child guess when the events occurred.)
2. Have each student choose which seven pictures to include. Tell them to pick at least two about which they remember something interesting (e.g., a funny story about learning to swing).
3. Distribute the student copies of the graphic organizer. Have the students paste their pictures in chronological order on the graphic organizer and then color them.
4. On a separate paper, have your students write the recitation of facts. Next, have them rewrite it including their anecdotes.

Day 3

1. Pair students; have them read their autobiographies to each other. Partners may suggest improvements. Have the students produce final drafts and attach them to the time lines.

Writing

Dear Parents:

We are creating autobiographies. Please tell your child the age at which he or she reached each milestone shown below. Have your child write the age above the box for each picture. For simplicity's sake, write ages in whole or half years, such as 4 years or 2½ years. For example, if your child walked at the age of 10 months, round it to 1 year.

Your child will use the time line to write a simple autobiography. Please return this page tomorrow. Thank you!

age:	age:	age:
swam	fed self with spoon or fork	went to school
age:	age:	age:
dressed self	read a book alone	lost first tooth
age:	age:	age:
pumped a swing	rode a bike	tied shoes

Writing

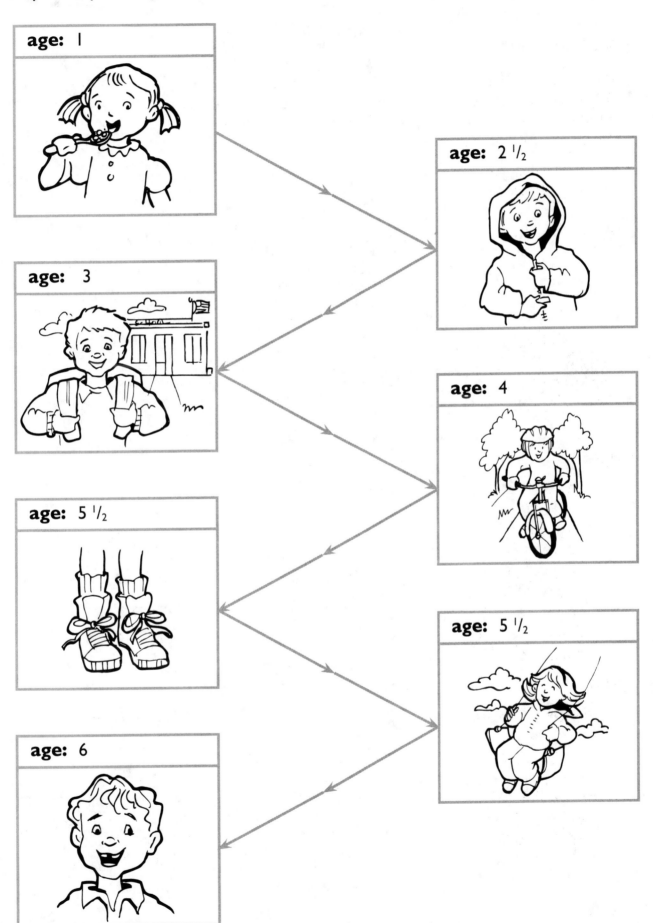

Writing

Day 1

1. Many writers think about and sketch out plot lines before they ever put pen to paper or their fingers on a keyboard. Students should do the same; this lesson will teach them how.

2. Make an overhead transparency and copies of the "If/Then Web" organizer on page 96.

3. Write this story on the board or on chart paper:

   Lily walked along the beach. She picked up seashells and put them into her pail.
   Suddenly she spotted an old wooden chest. It was wedged between two big rocks.
   It seemed to have washed up on the shore.

4. Have the students read the paragraph aloud chorally. Ask if anyone has any questions about the meaning of any of the words.

5. Display the overhead transparency and distribute the student copies.

6. Explain that most writers think about and "map out" the story line before they start writing a fiction scene. They do this by asking themselves, "If this happens, then what? If that occurs, then what next?" Remind your students that in every story there is at least one main character and a problem.

7. Write "Lily" in the first triangle. Write "old chest" in the other triangle. Instruct the students to do so at their seats.

8. Ask your students to brainstorm three things that Lily could do. Then ask them to brainstorm three problems that could occur with the chest. Write their ideas in the ovals.

9. Show your students the "story line" by saying "Lily could" and reading each of her options.

10. Show them the "problem" by saying, "The chest could" and reading each potential problem.

11. Ask your students to think even further down the line. What could happen in each case? Fill in this information in the boxes.

12. Read down each line, saying, "Lily could . . . and then . . ." Also read down each line, saying "The old chest could . . . and then . . ."

Day 2

1. As a class, decide which of the story lines work together the best. Then, let the students direct you in writing the story based on the story line chosen.

2. Compose the story on a blank overhead transparency. Keep it brief—no more than 10 lines. This is a fiction scene, not a whole story. It can have a cliffhanger ending.

Day 3

1. Make and distribute new student copies of the "If/Then Web" graphic organizer.

2. Make student copies of "Story Lines" on page 94. Each story line on the page is written at a first-grade reading level.

3. Instruct your students to choose the story line they like the best. They use it to fill in the organizer.

4. Collect these graphic organizers to check for understanding.

Day 4

1. Return the students' completed graphic organizers and have them write their scenes.

Writing

Story Lines

Kara moved closer to the pond's edge and parted the cattails. She wanted to find that frog.
Just then she felt her feet start to slip.

     •   •   •   •   •

Todd and Shane were riding their bikes. Suddenly, a big dog ran after them barking loudly.

     •   •   •   •   •

Jessica stumbled through the rain. It was falling so fast she could hardly see. Thunder
crashed and the ground shook. Lightning flashed. Where was that cabin?

     •   •   •   •   •

Sean leaped over the hole. He ran toward the chain-link fence. He quickly climbed it and
paused at the top. He looked back over his shoulder. They were still after him. In fact, they
were getting closer!

     •   •   •   •   •

Quickly, Tom started to reel in his line. The fish tugged and pulled hard. Tom struggled to
stay in the boat and not be pulled over the side. At last his catch came into view. He had
snagged a snapping turtle!

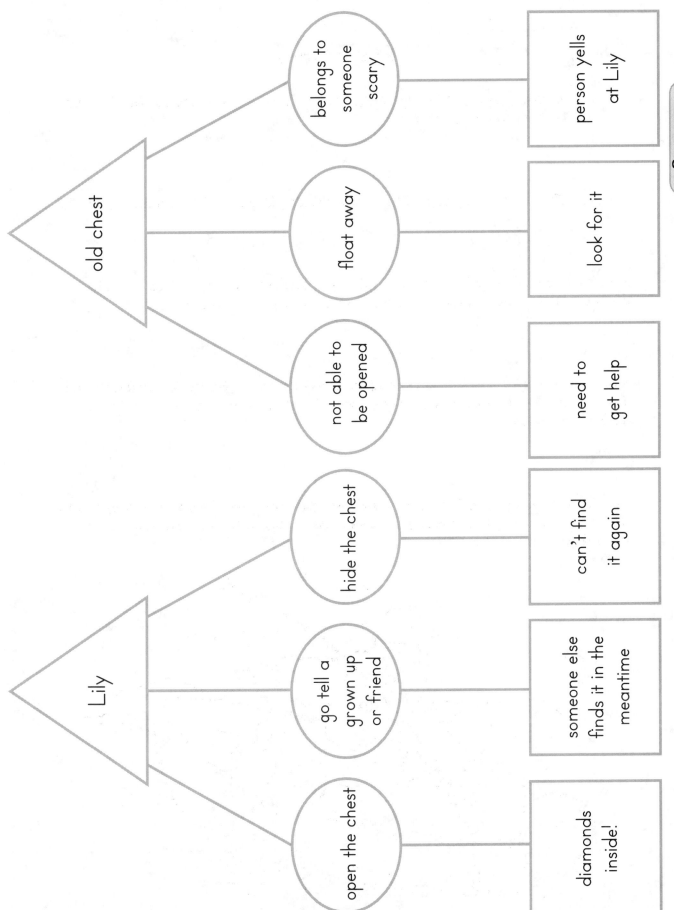

old chest

- belongs to someone scary — person yells at Lily
- float away — look for it
- not able to be opened — need to get help

Lily

- hide the chest — can't find it again
- go tell a grown up or friend — someone else finds it in the meantime
- open the chest — diamonds inside!

Writing